AFCA's
OFFENSIVE FOOTBALL
Drills

AMERICAN FOOTBALL COACHES ASSOCIATION

Human Kinetics

Library of Congress Cataloging-in-Publication Data

American Football Coaches Association.
  AFCA's offensive football drills / American Football Coaches
Association.
    p.   cm.
  ISBN 0-88011-526-2
  1. Football--Offense.   2. Football--Coaching.   3. Football-
-Training.   I. Title.
  GV951.8.A54   1998
  796.332'2--dc21   97-26550
                                                            CIP

ISBN: 0-88011-526-2

Content Editor: Dee Hawkes; **Managing Editor:** Coree Schutter; **Assistant Editor:** Laura Hambly; **Copyeditor:** Bonnie Pettifor; **Proofreader:** Kathy Bennett; **Graphic Designer:** Robert Reuther; **Graphic Artist:** Sandra Meier; **Photo Editor:** Boyd LaFoon; **Cover Designer:** Jack Davis; **Photographer (cover):** AllSport/Todd Warshaw; **Line Art Illustrator:** Keith Blomberg; **Mac Art Illustrator:** Craig Ronto; **Printer:** Versa Press

Human Kinetics books are available at special discounts for bulk purchase. Special editions or book excerpts can also be created to specification. For details, contact the Special Sales Manager at Human Kinetics.

Printed in the United States of America

10   9   8   7   6   5   4   3   2   1

Human Kinetics
Web site: http://www.humankinetics.com/

United States: Human Kinetics
P.O. Box 5076, Champaign, IL 61825-5076
1-800-747-4457
e-mail: humank@hkusa.com

Canada: Human Kinetics
Box 24040, Windsor, ON N8Y 4Y9
1-800-465-7301 (in Canada only)
e-mail: humank@hkcanada.com

Europe: Human Kinetics
P.O. Box IW14, Leeds LS16 6TR, United Kingdom
(44) 1132 781708
e-mail: humank@hkeurope.com

Australia: Human Kinetics
57A Price Avenue, Lower Mitcham, South Australia 5062
(088) 277 1555
e-mail: humank@hkaustralia.com

New Zealand: Human Kinetics
P.O. Box 105-231, Auckland 1
(09) 523 3462
e-mail: humank@hknewz.com

Contents

Foreword

Lights, camera, action! In an era when throwing the ball for a three-yard gain is considered more creative and exciting than a three-yard running play, it's no surprise that offenses across the country are going "show time."

While passing the ball may be the trendy and attention-getting style of play, what coaches, players, and fans are discovering is that a good, consistent passing attack first requires a principled philosophy and solid fundamentals, not simply a fancy playbook and a strong-armed quarterback. Essentially, what makes a running offense successful also makes a passing offense successful: sound technique and proper execution of timely plays performed by capable, motivated, and well-coached athletes.

AFCA's Offensive Football Drills is the best collection of position-specific and team offensive drills available in one resource. The American Football Coaches Association is grateful to the 75 high school and college coaches who contributed to this fine book.

If you play or coach a specific position, you'll find a chapter of drills just for you. When you want to put all of the pieces together to improve the performance of the entire offensive unit, work on the drills in chapter 5.

The AFCA believes that instructional resources like this drill book, which was developed by AFCA member coaches, serve a valuable function in the coaching profession and the sport of football. I encourage you to refer to it and use it often.

Grant Teaff
Executive Director, AFCA

Introduction

Much has been said and written about football's evolution from a running game to a pass-oriented attack. And it's a fact that teams throw the ball more today than they did 30 or 40 years ago. The Green Bay Packers, for example, amassed the team's four all-time highest season totals for rushing yardage from 1961 through 1964. In 1995, however, Green Bay gained more than three times the yards by passing the football as they did running it. A similar switch from running to passing occurred at the college level. In 1974 Ohio State ran the ball for 4,188 yards; in 1995 the Buckeyes threw for 3,490 yards.

Why the attraction to the passing game? Several reasons. For one, rule changes have made it easier to get receivers off the line of scrimmage and into the open field. Two, players and fans enjoy a more wide-open offense, so TV executives and football administrators at the pro and college levels have encouraged throwing the ball to keep interest high in the game. Three, failed attempts (remember the run-and-shoot?) to develop a productive, consistent passing attack led to the so-called West Coast offense, which proved that pass-first teams can win big season after season.

What the last four decades of football really tell us is that it doesn't matter so much whether you run or pass, as long as you develop a sound system, teach it well, and execute. That's why this book, *AFCA's Offensive Football Drills*, is such a valuable teaching tool. With its drills, position by position and then as a team, players can hone the very skills they will need to excel in competition.

Emphasize the drills that best meet your needs, but try them all. As the saying goes, it's not so much what play you run but *how* you run it. And more often than not, it's the best-drilled athlete or team who comes out on top.

Drill Finder

Key to Diagrams

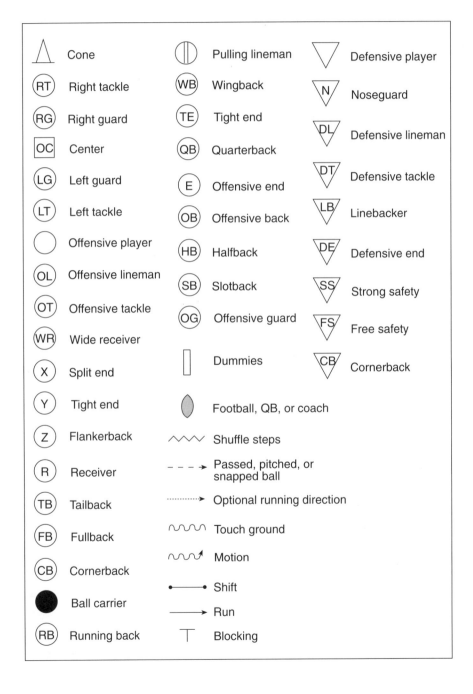

△ Cone	⊕ Pulling lineman	▽ Defensive player
RT Right tackle	WB Wingback	N Noseguard
RG Right guard	TE Tight end	DL Defensive lineman
OC Center	QB Quarterback	DT Defensive tackle
LG Left guard	E Offensive end	LB Linebacker
LT Left tackle	OB Offensive back	DE Defensive end
○ Offensive player	HB Halfback	SS Strong safety
OL Offensive lineman	SB Slotback	FS Free safety
OT Offensive tackle	OG Offensive guard	CB Cornerback
WR Wide receiver		
X Split end	▯ Dummies	
Y Tight end	⬮ Football, QB, or coach	
Z Flankerback	⌇⌇⌇ Shuffle steps	
R Receiver	– – – → Passed, pitched, or snapped ball	
TB Tailback	⋯⋯→ Optional running direction	
FB Fullback	∿∿∿ Touch ground	
CB Cornerback	∿∿∿↗ Motion	
● Ball carrier	•——• Shift	
RB Running back	——→ Run	
	⊤ Blocking	

PART 1
Offensive Line Drills

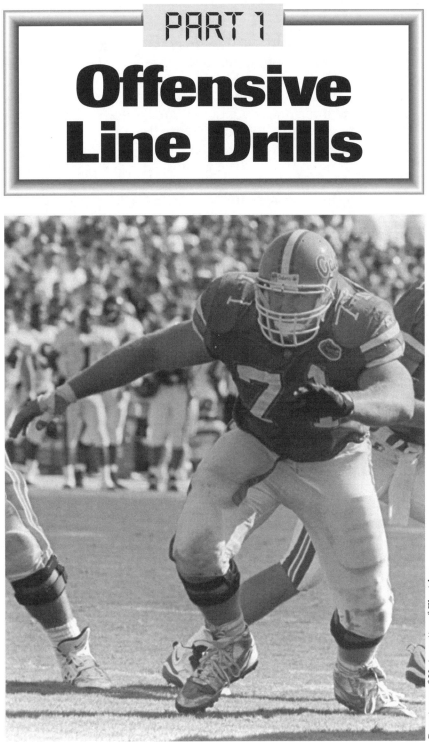

reat offensive teams start with great offensive lines. When the running game dominated college football, perennial powers like Nebraska, Michigan, Alabama, Southern California, Texas, Ohio State, and Oklahoma bulldozed their way down the field for one touchdown after another. Today, programs like Colorado, Florida State, Brigham Young, and Syracuse present multidimensional attacks, striking through the air more often than on the ground. The powers of the past and those of the present all have great offensive lines.

A successful offensive lineman in today's game has size, power, agility, and intelligence. He must also have a tremendous work ethic to stay motivated and keep practicing, despite receiving little notice from fans or the media. For example, for every Orlando Pace in the limelight, 50 other offensive linemen go unnoticed—until they miss a block.

Hard-working, team-oriented linemen are tremendous assets to an offense. The 18 drills presented in this section of the book will help hone the offensive lineman's technique and tactics. These drills will also make practice more fun, challenging, and productive for the men in the trenches.

Build a solid foundation for offensive success with a strong offensive line. Remember—the "skill position" athletes aren't going anywhere without good blocking.

Offensive Line Drills

Drill		Coach	Team
1	Crossfield	George Belu	Wake Forest
2	Strain	George DeLeone	San Diego Chargers
3	Recovery	Roger French	Brigham Young
4	Mirror Dodge	Steve Greatwood	St. Louis Rams
5	Cone	Joe Hollis	Arkansas State
6	Middle	Bret Ingalls	Northern Iowa
7	Recognition Period	James L. Jones	Justin Kimball H.S. (TX)
8	Second Effort	Whitey Jordan	Clemson
9	Combination	Bill Kroenke	Pittsburg State (KS)
10	Stance and Starts	Steven Loney	Iowa State
11	Knee	Gene McKeehan	U.S. Naval Academy
12	Counter Gap Read	Brent Myers	Northern Arizona
13	Chute	Scott Ricardo	Humboldt State
14	Intercept Pass Rush	Golden Ruel	Formerly with Kansas
15	Acceleration	Martin Schaetzle	Bucknell University
16	Slide and Punch	Jimmy Ray Stephens	Florida
17	Pin, Pull, and Trap	Milt Tenopir	Nebraska
18	Wall Up	John Wright	Hampton University

1   Crossfield

Coach: George Belu
Team: Wake Forest University
Head Coach: Jim Caldwell

Purpose: To teach players backside release and proper angles for downfield blocking.

Procedure:

1. On both sides of the field, place three stand-up dummies, two yards apart, forming an angle from the end of the bag near the line of scrimmage downfield toward the middle.
2. Align an offensive line, including the TE, on the line of scrimmage with a cone in front of each player.
3. On command, the right side (RG, RT, and TE) takes the proper release angle and sprints left, using the proper angle to execute a cross-body block to the appropriate bag. Then the blockers roll three times.
4. The blockers return to their feet and jog back to their original positions.
5. Next, the left side (OC, LG, and LT) repeats the procedure to its right.

Key Points:

- On approaching the bag, each blocker gets as close as possible, then executes a cross-body block, releasing off his feet into the bag (head and shoulders in front of bag).
- The blocker's proper first step is at a 45-degree angle with his inside foot.
- Insist that each blocker hustle and stay flat to the line of scrimmage while running the proper angle to his assigned bag.
- Emphasize that each blocker throws a block and then rolls three times.
- After the drill, the blocker must reposition the stand-up bag.

Crossfield

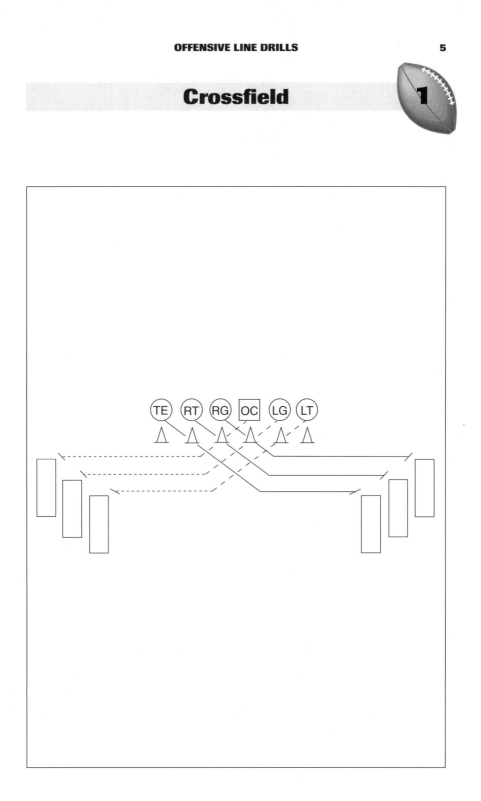

2 Strain

Coach: George DeLeone
Team: San Diego Chargers
Head Coach: Kevin Gilbride

Purpose: To simulate a stalemate at a drive block's moment of contact.

Procedure:

1. The blocker aligns in the chute.
2. Two feet away, two defenders with shields bend over together, straddling a board.
3. On command, the blocker explodes out from under the chute to attack the two shields.
4. Coach the defenders to totally resist and stop the blocker's charge, creating the stalemate by halting the blocker's progress.
5. After three seconds, whistle to have the defenders release pressure and resistance, allowing the blocker to finish his block.

Key Points:

- Throughout the drill, the two defenders must keep their shields touching and stay bent over hip to hip, each with his inside foot up.
- Upon contact, the defenders must work to keep the blocker stopped prior to the command or whistle to relax resistance.
- During contact, the blocker must gain one more step, move the defenders, and finish his block.
- Teach the blocker to stay low with his back flat and face up throughout the drill.
- The board helps the blocker maintain a wide base during the drill.

Strain

3   Recovery

Coach: Roger French
Team: Brigham Young University
Head Coach: LaVell Edwards

Purpose: To teach blockers to recover after a defender changes his rush lane.

Procedure:

1. The drill station is a five-yard square with a cone (QB) placed in the middle of the back line.
2. A blocker sets up near the front line of the square.
3. A defender faces the blocker in an offset position (right or left).
4. On command, the defender attempts to rush (touch) the QB (cone), while the blocker attempts to stop him from getting upfield.
5. Upon being stopped, the defender spins or clubs back in a change of direction.

Key Points:

- The blocker must move the defender laterally or diagonally, not bail out.
- While protecting, the blocker must not cross his feet.
- This drill teaches the blocker not to overplay the defense.
- By emphasizing correct footwork, the blocker gets a feel both for executing the proper cutoff position and for changes of direction by the defender.
- The importance of recovery is stressed when the defender changes direction.

Recovery

3

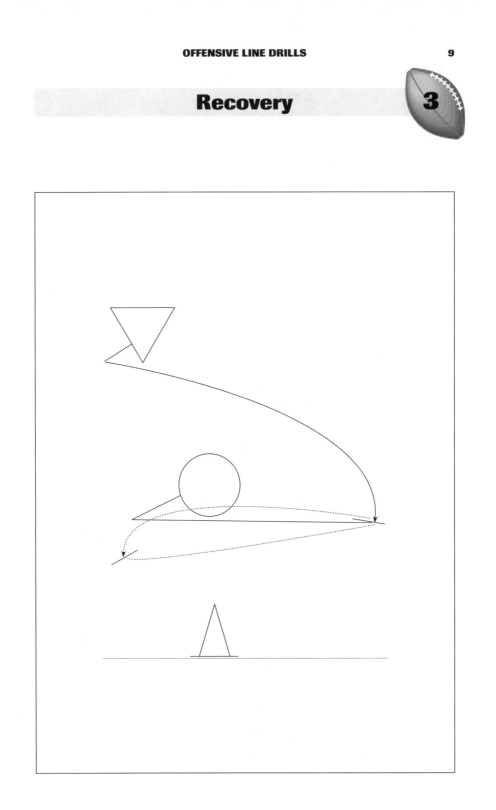

Mirror Dodge

Coach: Steve Greatwood
Team: St. Louis Rams
Head Coach: Dick Vermeil

Purpose: To enhance lateral mobility, balance, and body control.

Procedure:

1. Place two cones on a line, five to six yards apart.
2. The blocker aligns himself between the cones with his heels in front of the line.
3. The defender faces the blocker about a yard and a half away.
4. On command, the defender uses quick movements to penetrate the line and then circles around either cone.
5. The blocker "mirrors" the defender by blocking him so he cannot cross the line.
6. If the defender scores (by circling a cone), he keeps circling the cone until the blocker aligns in front of the defender again.
7. Rotate two new players in after 10 to 12 seconds.

Key Points:

- The defender must use quickness, and not a hard rush, to score.
- The blocker keeps his head in front of the line, his shoulders square, and his hips under in order to keep good posture and balance.
- Conduct this competitive drill at full speed and challenge the blocker by having quicker players such as DBs, WRs, and RBs be the defender.
- Widen the cones to eight to nine yards apart as the blocker develops his skill.
- Variation: Put two-on-two with the cones eight to nine yards apart to switch-block the twist stunt and work on peripheral vision.

Mirror Dodge

4

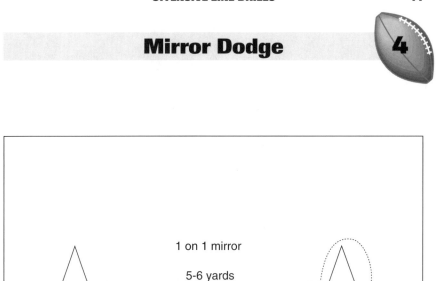

1 on 1 mirror

5-6 yards

A

B

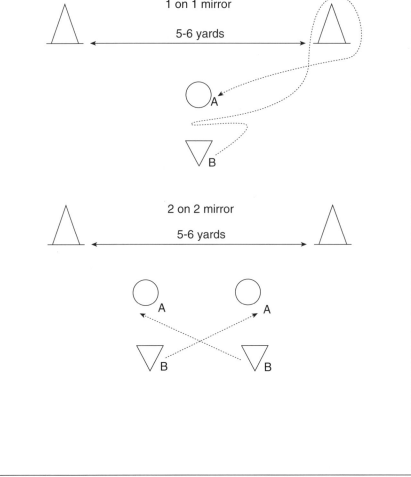

2 on 2 mirror

5-6 yards

A   A

B   B

5   **Cone**

Coach: Joe Hollis
Team: Arkansas State University
Head Coach: Joe Hollis

Purpose: To teach linemen proper blocking stance, footwork, and hand use while pass protecting.

Procedure:

1. Place two cones seven yards apart on a line.
2. A blocker aligns in the middle three yards in front of the cones.
3. A defender aligns head-up on the blocker.
4. On command, the defender rushes the cone while the blocker attempts to keep him outside the cone.
5. Once the defender passes the cone, the blocker sprints back to the starting point.

Key Points:

- To condition the blocker, the blocker gets in as many repetitions as possible in 15 seconds (three or four).
- The blocker must keep a good base in a bent-knee position and shuffle his feet without crossing them over.
- The blocker keeps his hands and arms free by not grabbing hold of the defender in rerouting the defender past the cone.
- The blocker should anticipate the defender's moves and be ready to block them.

Cone

5

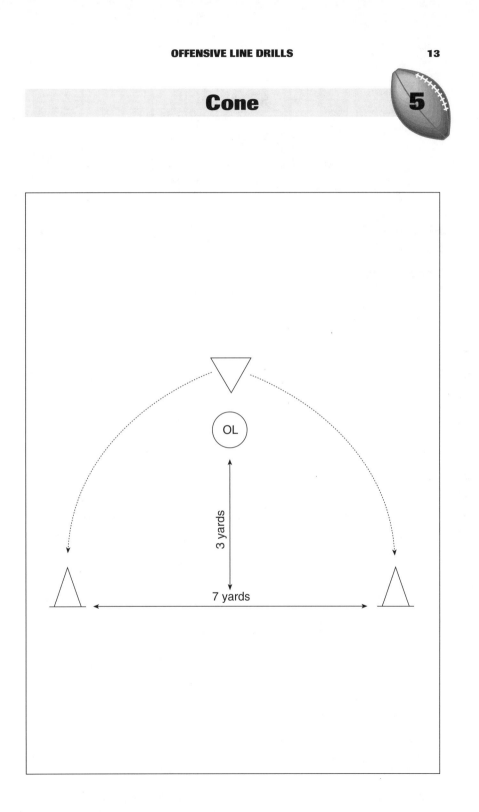

6

Middle

Coach: Bret Ingalls
Team: Northern Iowa University
Head Coach: Mike Dunbar

Purpose: To teach the fundamentals of combination (zone) blocks.

Procedure:

1. Set up two teaching stations at the line of scrimmage:
   a. Align OC, RG, and LG with QB versus two DTs and MLB in 4-3 defense (diagram 1).
   b. Align OT and TE versus OLB and DE (diagram 2).
2. On QB cadence, group #1 zone-blocks either to the right or left.
3. On QB cadence, group #2 either scoop-blocks the back-side or zone-blocks the frontside.
4. Before switching, each group executes three blocking calls.

Key Points:

- Always check each lineman for proper alignment.
- Teach linemen to demonstrate good footwork and always keep a solid base.
- Upon contact, lineman must keep their legs driving.
- Once the players understand the drill, the defense can adjust and run movements.
- Make this drill part of every offensive practice plan.

Middle

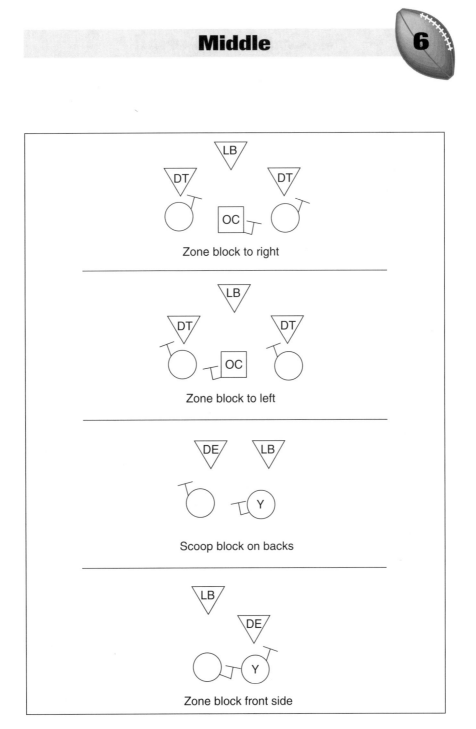

Zone block to right

Zone block to left

Scoop block on backs

Zone block front side

7   **Recognition Period**

Coach: James L. Jones
Team: Justin Kimball High School (Texas)
Head Coach: James L. Jones

Purpose: To teach young offensive linemen to recognize different defensive fronts.

Procedure:

1. The offensive line, including TEs, aligns on the ball.
2. Place seven large plastic trash cans as defensive players in front.
3. The coach stands behind the offensive line with a script of plays.
4. On command, the offensive linemen come off the ball to block their areas.
5. Conduct the drill by changing the defense (trash cans) from an even to an odd front.

Key Points:

- Teach the offensive linemen to start from a balanced stance.
- Check for proper steps as each lineman moves to block.
- When executing the blocking skill, the linemen should use a punch technique first.
- The drill is over when the offensive line has correctly blocked the plays off the script.

Recognition Period

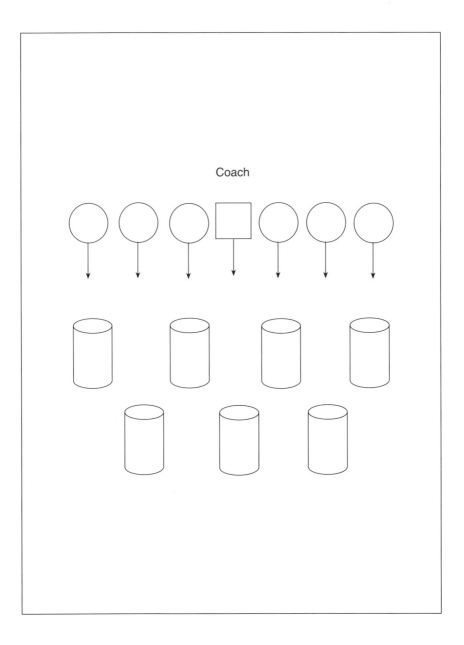

Coach

Second Effort

Coach: Whitey Jordan
Team: Clemson University
Head Coach: Tommy West

Purpose: To teach linemen the importance of making a second effort.

Procedure:

1. Place five eight-foot-long boards, five yards apart, perpendicular to the line of scrimmage.
2. Position a defensive player holding a stand-up dummy near the front end of each board.
3. Place a dummy downfield at the end of each board.
4. On the snap count, blocker drive-blocks the defender off the board.
5. After the drive block, blocker seat-rolls, gets up, and blocks the downfield dummy.
6. At the end of the drill, the blocker trades roles with the defender.

Key Points:

- The player holding stand-up dummy resists, then steps straight back.
- The blocker must block full speed and do perfect seat rolls to both the right and left.
- Emphasize correct stance and proper drive block fundamentals.
- To be more competitive, use additional downfield dummies.

Second Effort

8

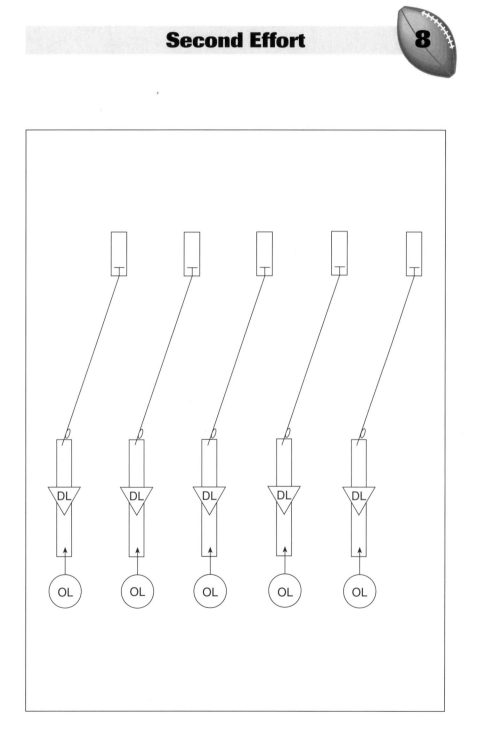

Combination

Coach: Bill Kroenke
Team: Pittsburg State University (Kansas)
Head Coach: Chuck Broyles

Purpose: To practice running play combination blocks versus defensive shade techniques.

Procedure:

1. Set up three groups of blockers five yards apart (see diagram) to drill on the same line of scrimmage and include the QB with the OC.

2. Position three defenders (two DTs and a DE, each against a different group of blockers) in a shade technique.

3. One coach stands in front of the blockers to signal play selection, direction, and snap count by hand or with cards. Another coach stands behind the blockers to signal defenders as to the defensive alignment.

4. The QB sounds cadence, and on the snap count, each group of blockers execute their combination blocks.

Key Points:

- Outline the drill and expectations at a meeting prior to the drill so players understand what they are going to do before taking the field.

- All groups work in the same direction and off the same snap count.

- Each group switches after the third repetition.

- Emphasize matching competitive blockers and defenders.

- Film the drill from behind the offense.

- This drill allows for game-like conditions with less chance of injury.

Combination

9

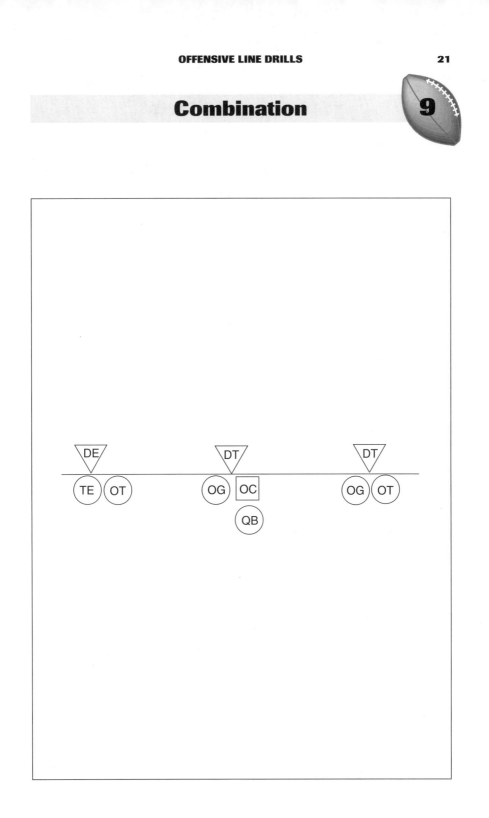

10   **Stance and Starts**

Coach: Steven Loney
Team: Iowa State University
Head Coach: Dan McCarney

Purpose: To teach offensive linemen the proper pre-set stance and steps on reach blocks and backside cutoffs.

Procedure:

1. Using a line spacer, place three eight-foot-long boards parallel to each other.
2. Each offensive lineman aligns in a three-point stance in the middle of the board, setting up his outside foot in the middle of the board.
3. At the end of each board, align a defender holding a shield.
4. On the starting count, each blocker fires out by driving off the up foot, replacing his down hand with his back foot on the first step.
5. Each blocker sprints to the end of his board to make contact with the defender.
6. Upon contact, the defender escapes, forcing the blocker to drive his outside knee upfield.

Key Points:

- Teach the blocker to keep his head up and back flat, to drive his arms, and to keep a wide base.
- Adjust the spacing of the defenders, depending upon the defensive alignments expected from the next opponent.
- Before the drill starts, check each blocker's pre-set stance.
- The coach may have all blockers come off together.

Stance and Starts

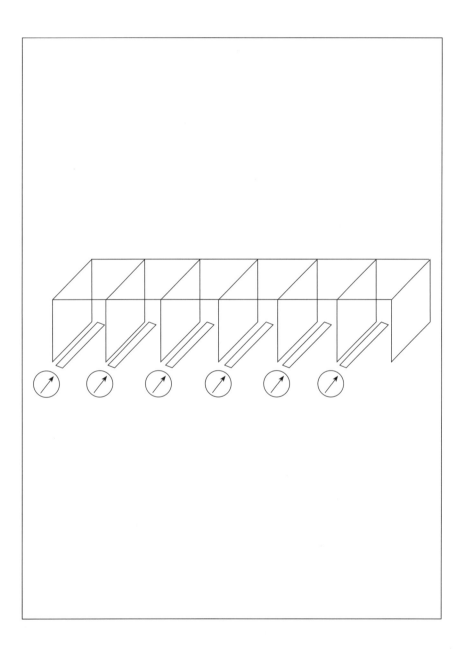

11

Knee

Coach: Gene McKeehan
Team: United States Naval Academy
Head Coach: Charlie Weatherbie

Purpose: To teach an offensive lineman the feel of his hips moving under him, giving him proper leverage with a good pad level.

Procedure:

1. The offensive line straddles a yard line, facing the coach.
2. On the command "hit," each player takes a short (six-inch) step straight ahead with his right foot.
3. As the player takes his short step, his left knee rolls forward and touches the ground without crossing the line he is straddling.
4. As the left knee touches the ground, the player pushes off with his left foot and rolls his hips under him while moving forward.
5. Continue the motion by repeating steps 2 through 4, but stepping with the left foot.

Key Points:

- During the drill, the player must keep his feet and knees straddling the line.
- This movement will force him to take short, choppy steps to keep his balance.
- The player's knee must roll forward and not drop to the ground.
- The player's knee must not touch the line, so his hips keep going forward.
- Run the drill until the player gets the feel of his hips moving under him.
- Have other players yell "Get good pad level!" to ensure a focus point.

Knee

- Variation: Add a defender with a hand bag. The player makes contact with the bag after pushing off from the knee.

12   Counter Gap Read

Coach: Brent Myers
Team: Northern Arizona University
Head Coach: Steve Axman

Purpose: To teach the backside pulling OG, OT, and TE to read which defenders to block while on the move.

Procedure:

1. Place one large blocking dummy perpendicular to the line of scrimmage, opposite where the OC would align.
2. Set up two stations: (1) LG and LT or TE running the drill to the right, and (2) RG and RT or TE running the drill to the left.
3. Position a DE and inside LB on the side of the dummy away from the blockers, each holding a hand shield.
4. Align in front of the defenders and away from the blockers to signal defensive movements.
5. At each station, the backside OG pulls to either kickout-block an upfield DE or log-block a DE who is closing the hole.
6. At each station, the backside OT or TE pulls to lead-block the LB.

Key Points:

- Teach the OT or TE to feel and read the block of the OG in order to effectively block the LB on his pursuit angle.
- The coach signals the DE to either get upfield or close the trap lane and tells the LB to stay in the hole or scrape over the top of the DE.
- Use the blocking dummy to simulate the pile that occurs at the point of a double-team block.
- The blocking dummy also simulates a down block on either a three- or one-technique defender, so when a trap occurs the OG can pull up tight to kickout-block the LB.

Counter Gap Read

12

- Correct each blocker to improve coordinated counter gap blocking.

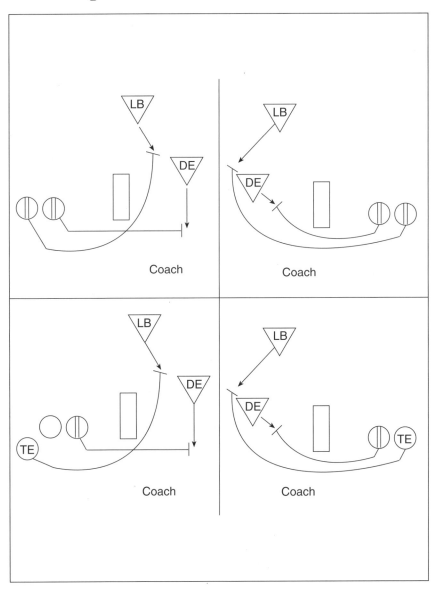

Chute

Coach: Scott Ricardo
Team: Humboldt State
Head Coach: Fred Whitmire

Purpose: To teach and develop proper blocking techniques by staying low.

Procedure:

1. The chute is 18 feet long, 42 inches high, and divided into six three-foot-wide stations.
2. Align one blocker and one defender in each station.
3. Teach each phase of blocking by progressive steps:
    a. One-step technique: The blocker steps forward, throwing his arms back to his hips.
    b. Two-step technique: The blocker whips his arms forward and punches on the second step.
    c. Three-step technique: The blocker rolls his hips forward, and drives forward.
4. Each blocker faces his defender and executes the called block.

Key Points:

- One-step technique: Correct overstriding and check for a flat back.
- Two-step technique: Listen to hear the "pop" sound coming from the punch.
- Three-step technique: Emphasize the roll of each player's hips with fast choppy feet while maintaining a solid base.
- On heavy contact days, conduct the drill live against LBs.
- This drill helps the blocker stay low on his initial movement to maintain a stronger blocking angle.
- In the final challenge of the year, allow seniors to pick whomever they want to go live against. The more excited the coach during the one-on-one confrontations, the better the drill.

Chute

14 Intercept Pass Rush

Coach: Golden Ruel
Team: Formerly with University of Kansas

Purpose: To teach linemen the proper intercept point to the QB and how to intercept a defender.

Procedure:

1. The LT, LG, OC, RG, and RT line up on the line of scrimmage in correct stances.
2. Draw a dotted intercept line, 10 yards deep, behind each tackle.
3. Put defenders ready to rush the QB from different angles opposite each blocker.
4. Line up the QB directly behind the OC, 8 yards deep.
5. To implement pass protection ensure the following:

   a. Guards and tackles work together.

   b. Center and guards work together.
6. On ball movement, blockers recognize the angle of the defender and block him.

Key Points:

- Tackles work on pass sets against inside, head-up, five-, seven-, or nine-technique defenders.
- Guards work on pass sets against inside, head-up, and three-technique defenders.
- Center works on head-up or gap defenders.
- The center and guards set, stay square, and work the intercept point by keeping their defenders on the line of scrimmage.
- Against a wide-rush defender, the tackle stays on the intercept line by staying as deep as he is wide. The tackle must pivot to the outside when facing a wide-rush defender, not turn his shoulders on the drop.

Intercept Pass Rush　14

- Insist that all blockers stay inside conscious, work with bent knees, keep their heads up, keep their backs vertical, and slide with a solid base.
- To avoid collisions, have all defenders work from the same side.

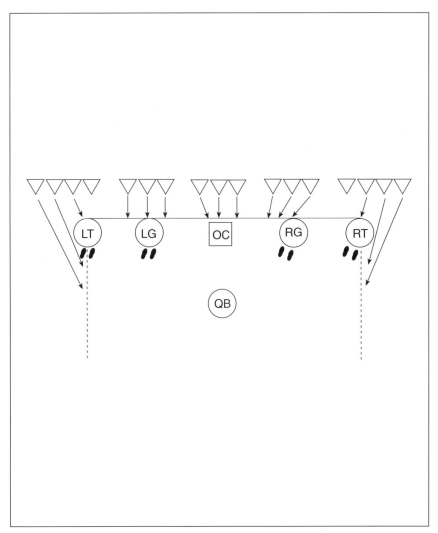

15 Acceleration

Coach: Martin Schaetzle
Team: Bucknell University
Head Coach: Tom Gadd

Purpose: To teach linemen the importance of accelerating and moving their feet upon contact.

Procedure:

1. To teach the blocker to accelerate his feet, use a three-man sled.
2. The blocker aligns in good two-point football stance head up in front of the sled.
3. The blocker's feet are close enough to the sled to explode into a "fit" position.
4. On command, the blocker explodes into the sled with his blocking surface and continues accelerating his feet until the sled returns to the ground.

Key Points:

- Using the proper blocking surface (two-hand drive and forearm rip), the blocker rolls his hips to lift the sled.
- Remind the blocker rolling his hips is much like his off-season strength program of power cleans and squats.
- Upon contact, the blocker's feet must accelerate.
- The blocker must keep a wide base.
- Emphasize that the blocker must keep moving his feet throughout the drill.

Acceleration

16   Slide and Punch

Coach: Jimmy Ray Stephens
Team: University of Florida
Head Coach: Steve Spurrier

Purpose: To teach linemen in pass protection to time their punch (jam) as they shuffle and mirror the defender.

Procedure:

1. A single file line of blockers faces another single file line of defenders.
2. On command, the blocker shuffles down the line of scrimmage, mirroring a defender.
3. After two or three steps, the defender steps forward into the blocker, simulating a pass rusher.
4. The blocker reacts to the defender by focusing on the target (between the numbers) and timing his punch. They continue down the line of scrimmage for 10 yards, repeating the rush-block two or three more times.
5. The next two in line start when the pair of players in front is five yards away.
6. Others in line follow the same sequence until all players have completed the drill.

Key Points:

- The blocker must keep his post foot up, use short shuffle steps, and maintain a wide base to ensure good balance.
- Emphasize that the blocker must maintain proper body posture:
  a. Bend at the knees.
  b. Keep the back straight and shoulders back.
  c. Keep elbows next to the rib cage.
  d. Keep hands inside (thumbs up) at the chest level.
- Stress the importance of focusing intensely on the target.

Slide and Punch

 16

- Coach the blocker to time his punch by striking an upward blow at the numbers, sitting, and separating.
- Teach the blocker to keep the defender's hands off him.

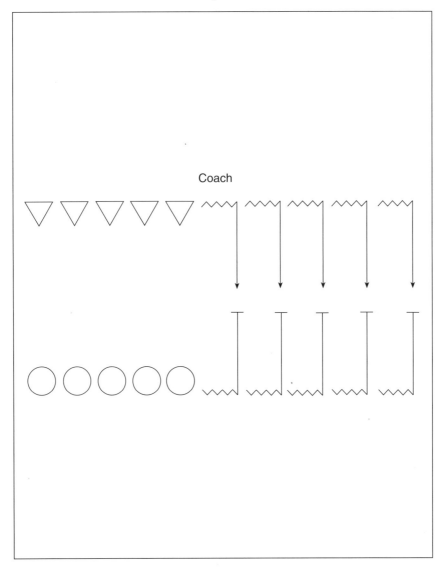

Coach

Pin, Pull, and Trap

Coach: Milt Tenopir
Team: University of Nebraska
Head Coach: Tom Osborne

Purpose: To teach linemen to down-block and pull- and trap-block in the open field.

Procedure:

1. Align four blockers in a straight line, each with an assigned number.

2. Place one large stand-up dummy (with holder) in front of #4 and another in front of #2. Place one air dummy (with holder) three to four yards in front of #1 and another air dummy outside #1 and on the line.

3. On command, blockers #1 and #3 step at a 45-degree angle and pin the stand-up dummies.

4. On command, blocker #2 pulls, climbs the line, and traps the end air dummy inside-out while blocker #4 pulls, reads the block of #2, and sprints through the upfield air dummy.

Key Points:

- Teach pulling blocker #2 that the first step is directional at a 45-degree angle, and the second step is a pull step, back into the line of scrimmage. The second step is never parallel to the line of scrimmage.

- The type of play called will determine the aiming point for #1 and #3 when blocking down to pin.

- The defender holding the upfield air dummy should retreat upon contact by #4.

- Blocker #4 strikes air dummy with his hands in an upward motion to develop a lift.

- After contact, blocker #4 is to sprint through the defender rather than deliver one shot and stop.

- Use different plays and go both directions.

Pin, Pull, and Trap

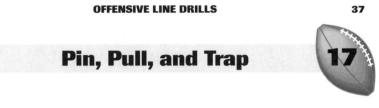

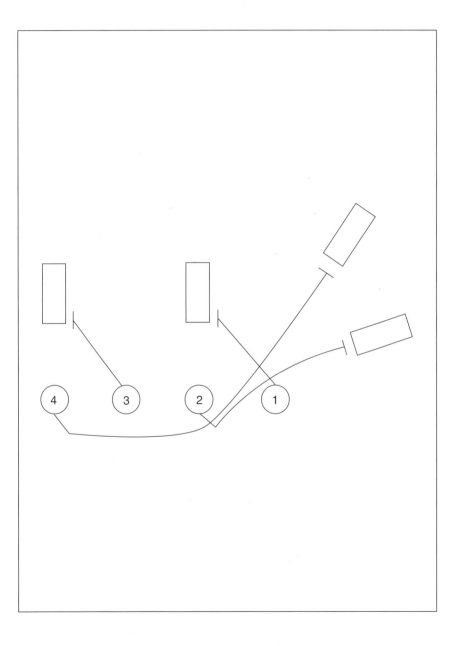

18

Wall Up

Coach: John Wright
Team: Hampton University
Head Coach: Joe Taylor

Purpose: To teach a pulling guard and tackle the proper path to take to block either a counter or power off-tackle play.

Procedure:

1. The guards form one line (#1) and the tackles form another line (#2). The lines are side by side, four feet apart, facing the coach.

2. Station #1: A player holds a stand-up dummy at a right angle, 10 yards from line #1.

3. Station #2: Place three flat bags on the ground. The first bag is at a 45-degree angle to the lines, the other two bags are back-to-back in line with the first bag. A player holds a stand-up dummy at the end of the third bag.

4. On the snap count, the first guard (line #1) pulls and kickout-blocks the stand-up dummy.

5. On the snap count, the first tackle (line #2) pulls and follows the path of the bags to block the stand-up dummy.

6. Players at each station rotate holding the dummy.

Key Points:

- Teach blockers to keep their heads up and use the proper shoulder when executing a block (the same shoulder as the direction the player is pulling).

- The #2 drill is designed to teach the blocker to stay close to the down block so he can effectively take on a scrape LB.

- Perform the drills in both directions, then switch the lines.

- Make sure each blocker keeps his head up and blocks only with his correct shoulder.

Wall Up

18

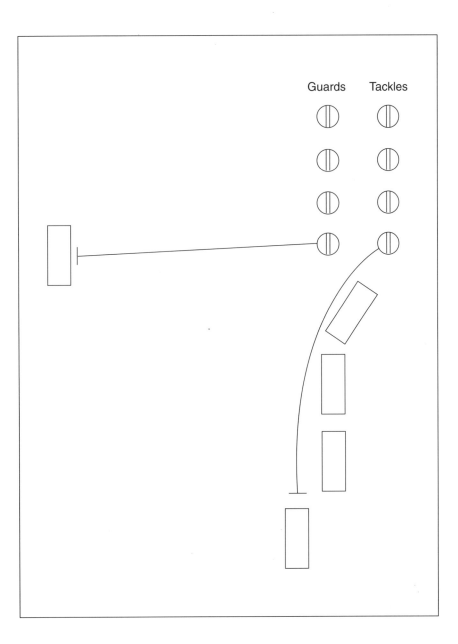

PART 2
Running Back Drills

No position carries more of the offensive load than the running back. A backfield workhorse can wear down a defense and open it up for later scores with play-action passes.

Many of the sport's all-time greats were running backs. Jim Thorpe, Jim Brown, and Walter Payton are only a select few. Their impact on a game is enormous; the opposing defense focuses its efforts on stopping the main backfield threat. Whether he's an elusive Gale Sayers, a bruising Earl Campbell, or a speed-power combination like Emmitt Smith, the dominant runner finds a way to gain yardage.

Although their skills may appear instinctive, great backs become great because they work harder. They train to peak physical condition. They learn each play so well that they know exactly where each block is to be made, and which teammate is assigned to make it. They work on their timing, their blocking, their pass receiving—always striving to become a complete back. And, because they know the damage caused by a turnover, they protect the football and refuse to fumble no matter how hard they're hit.

The drills in this section will help running backs develop these skills and attitudes. Run them so you know who's going to get the ball on third and two.

Running Back Drills

Drill	Coach	Team
19 Blitz Control	Stephen Bell	MacMurray College
20 Redbird Run	Todd Berry	Illinois State
21 Dip, Rip, and Score	Charles Coe	Memphis
22 Recovery	Larry Coker	Miami
23 Jump Cut	Bob DeBesse	Southwest Texas State
24 Read	Tony DeMeo	Washburn University
25 Cut and Go	Larry Fedora	U.S. Air Force Academy
26 Mat Low Block	Fran Ganter	Penn State
27 Da Bone	Walt Hunt	U. of Puget Sound
28 Hand Down Bag	Jud Keim	California Lutheran
29 Blast	Kelly Skipper	Fresno State
30 Hide-and-Seek	Don Treadwell	Stanford
31 Blitz Pickup	Bob Visger	California State–Sacramento

19   Blitz Control

Coach: Stephen Bell
Team: MacMurray College
Head Coach: Bob Frey

Purpose: To train RBs to identify blitz packages and recognize the differences in how to block different packages.

Procedure:

1. Align RBs in a specific backfield set (split, I, and so on). Use a stand-up dummy to simulate the QB.
2. Position LBs according to the offensive set called. They must be prepared to blitz.
3. On coach's command, the LBs attack either as a harder or softer blitzer.
4. Each RB executes a proper blitz check, recognizes the blitz technique used by the LBs, and blocks accordingly.

Key Points:

- This drill is set up for five-step drop passing game.
- Designate which LBs will blitz and how hard each blitzer comes.
- Teach the RB to attack a blitzer at the line of scrimmage.
- Teach the RB to chop-block a hard blitzer at the line of scrimmage and pass-protect a soft blitzer outside the pocket.
- To simulate game-like conditions, add a QB who drops back to pass.
- The RB must recognize his blitz check responsibility.

Blitz Control

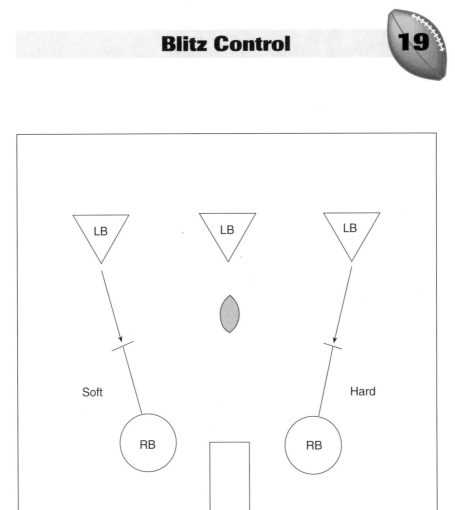

19

20   Redbird Run

Coach: Todd Berry
Team: Illinois State University
Head Coach: Todd Berry

Purpose: To teach RBs ball security, footwork, and leverage.

Procedure:

1. Place a set of running ropes on a straight line, five yards from a blaster.

2. One player (with the ball in his right arm) aligns at the end of the ropes. The remaining players take positions along both sides of the ropes.

3. The drill begins by having the ball carrier run through the ropes, while the players along the side attempt to strip the ball from his arm.

4. The ball carrier accelerates out of the ropes into the blaster.

5. As the ball carrier exits the blaster, signal him to make a directional cut.

6. The drill then continues with the next player in line.

Key Points:

- The ball carrier learns to carry the ball in either arm (ball security) while running through the ropes.

- The ball carrier must maintain proper pad leverage to exit the blaster successfully.

- While exiting the blaster, it is important for the ball carrier to keep his eyes up to make the correct directional cut.

- Variations:
  a. The ball carrier can enter the blaster first.
  b. Hand off or toss the ball to the ball carrier.
  c. To create additional cuts each RB will enter and exit the ropes at different angles.
  d. Have the ball carrier run different rope patterns.

Redbird Run

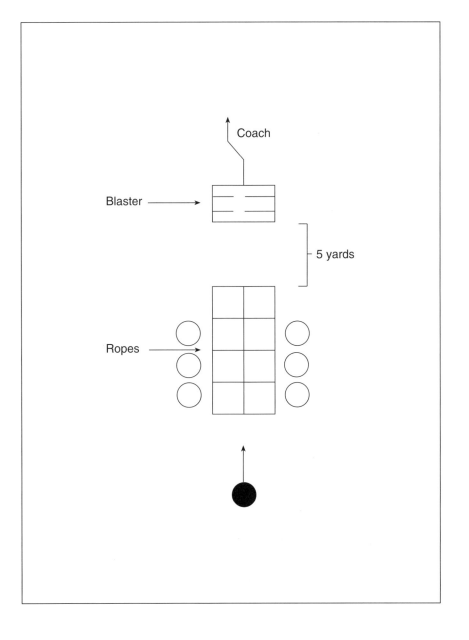

Coach

Blaster ————————▶

5 yards

Ropes ————————▶

21 Dip, Rip, and Score

Coach: Charles Coe
Team: University of Memphis
Head Coach: Rip Scherer

Purpose: To teach RBs the fundamentals of staying in bounds.

Procedure:

1. Position five defenders holding hand shields.
   a. Place the first three defenders near the sideline, one each at the 15-yard line, the 10-yard line, and the 5-yard line.
   b. Place two defenders standing side by side at the front end of the end zone on the goal line.
2. Set the ball carrier behind the QB at the 20-yard line hashmark.
3. On the snap, the QB either tosses or hands off to the ball carrier, who runs up the sideline.
4. The ball carrier runs past the three defenders as each one tries to force him out of bounds.
5. At the goal line, the ball carrier bursts between the two defenders to score.

Key Points:

- Insist that each RB warm up before entering the drill.
- Instruct sideline defenders to step toward the ball carrier, but not jam the back of the ball carrier's head.
- RBs start in the proper stance and carry the ball in the outside arm.
- Teach the RB to lower his shoulder (dip) and drive into each defender with an inside forearm (rip) shoulder blow.
- Conduct the drill on both hashmarks, including all ball carriers (RBs, QBs, TEs, and WRs).
- Start the drill at half speed, give each ball carrier two carries at each hashmark, and finish the drill at full speed.

Dip, Rip, and Score

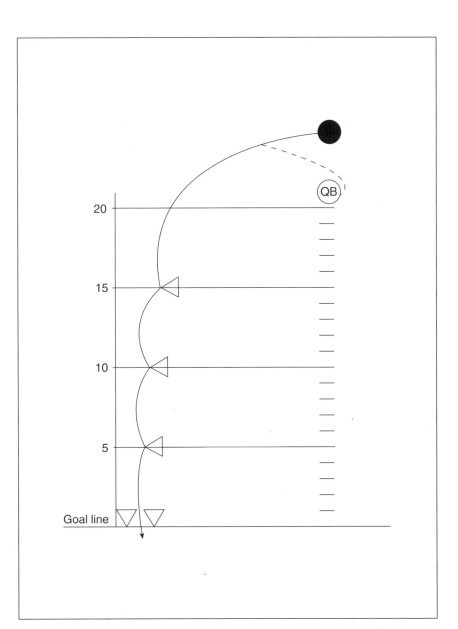

22   # **Recovery**

Coach: Larry Coker
Team: University of Miami
Head Coach: Butch Davis

Purpose: To teach proper balance, recovery, and changing of hands with the football while running.

Procedure:

1. Align two cones on a straight line, 10 yards apart. Form a triangle with a third cone.

2. RBs (with footballs) position themselves at an angle, 5 yards from the first cone.

3. On command, the first RB runs 3/4 speed to the first cone with the ball in his right hand. At the cone, he taps the turf twice with the palm of his left hand.

4. The RB gathers himself, switches the ball over to his left hand, and runs at 3/4 speed directly at the second cone. At that cone, he taps the turf twice with the palm of his right hand.

5. The RB gathers himself, switches the ball over to right hand, and repeats the procedure at the third (final) cone.

6. The RB gathers himself and finishes with a five-yard sprint.

Key Points:

- Carry the football with three pressure points: the rib cage, forearm, and hand.

- When changing hands, the RB must keep the ball in contact with his abdomen.

- Touch the turf with the palm of the off hand, not only the fingers.

- After each hand exchange, the RB must resume the proper ball carrying technique.

Recovery

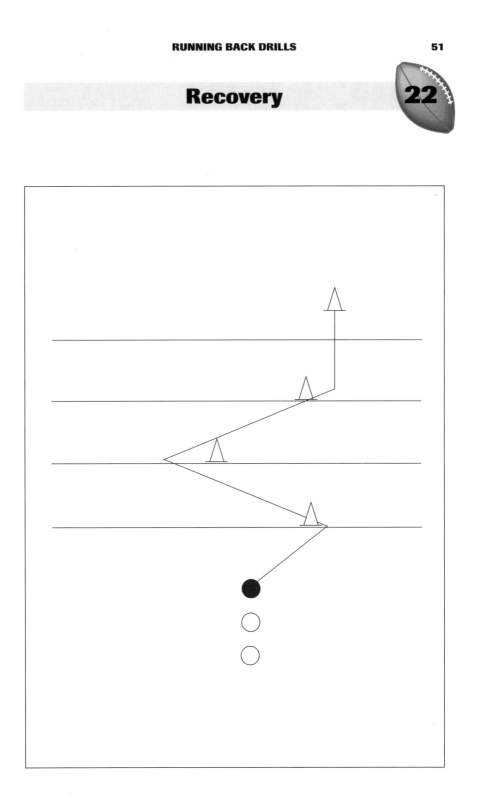

23   Jump Cut

Coach: Bob DeBesse
Team: Southwest Texas State University
Head Coach: Bob DeBesse

Purpose: To teach RBs to get upfield as quickly as possible, using quick feet and lateral moves.

Procedure:

1. Set up a cone to mark the starting line.
2. Place two flat dummies straight ahead, three yards apart, with the front end of each five yards from the starting line. Place a third flat dummy perpendicular to the left vertical dummy, touching the left dummy, to form an "L."
3. Place another flat dummy five yards further upfield, parallel to the start line, with the right end in line with the outside edge of the right vertical dummy. The coach stands behind this last dummy to signal.
4. Place a second cone five yards further upfield, centered on the upfield horizontal dummy.
5. Align ball carrier (with the ball) next to the starting cone.
6. On command, the ball carrier attacks the angle of the "L" of the front dummies, pops his feet with a hard plant, and jump-cuts parallel to the horizontal dummy.
7. The ball carrier then runs upfield and attacks the next horizontal dummy by getting on top of it, ready to jump-step opposite of the coach's movement.
8. After he completes the jump step, the ball carrier stays tight to the dummy, runs upfield, and accelerates through the last cone.

Key Points:

• Teach the ball carrier to go full speed when attacking each jump move.
• The second jump step simulates an open-field defender. Teach the ball carrier to step on his toes.

Jump Cut

- The ball carrier must finish the drill upfield at full speed.
- Use these key phases as appropriate: Bury yourself! Get upfield! Accelerate! Step on his toes! Finish it! Angles! Score!

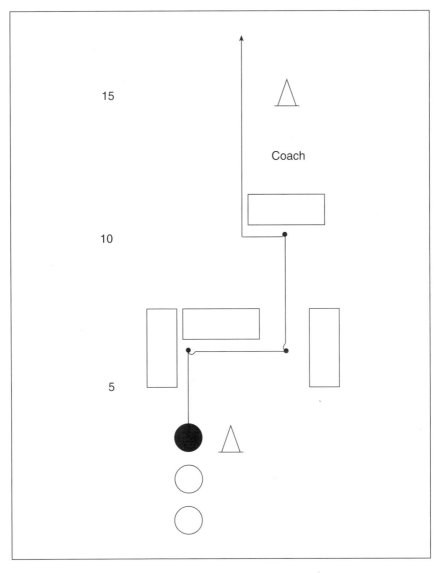

24 Read

Coach: Tony DeMeo
Team: Washburn University
Head Coach: Tony DeMeo

Purpose: To teach RBs and the QB in the triple-option offense how to react to different defensive looks.

Procedure:
1. At full speed, an option team (nine players) runs triple-option plays against a scout team (six players) into the sideline.
2. QB executes the triple option, reading the defense for the handoff key and the pitch key.
3. There is no huddle. The drill begins on the quick count of the QB, with the backs alternating and the line staying the same.
4. The QB coach signals to the defender that will react to the handoff and the pitchback.

Key Points:
- The scout team must align properly, then move toward the ball.
- Change defensive stunts every two plays.
- The goal for this high-tempo drill is to get 100 repetitions in 20 minutes.
- Coach on the move to run this drill effectively.

Read

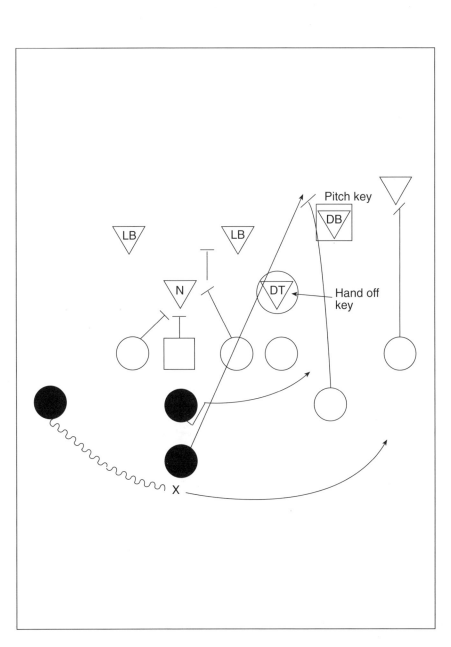

25   **Cut and Go**

Coach: Larry Fedora
Team: United States Air Force Academy
Head Coach: Fisher DeBerry

Purpose: To teach RBs open-field running skills.

Procedure:

1. Run this drill from the sideline toward the hashmark between 10-yard lines.
2. Place five cones in a line, one yard apart, directly in front of the first RB in line.
3. Place two cones inside the left yard line, 10 yards in from the sideline.
4. Beyond the yard line cones, position a player holding a heavy dummy.
5. The RBs align (with the ball) on the sideline in a single file, facing the cones.
6. On command, the RB (ball in right arm), starting on the left side of the first cone, weaves through all the cones.
7. After the last cone, the RB sprints to the right yard line, where he puts his left hand down on the ground, then turns around and runs toward the two yard line cones.
8. Upon reaching the cones, the RB turns upfield between the cones and rips through the dummy with his right arm and shoulder to finish sprinting through the hashmark.

Key Points:

- Throughout the drill, the RB secures the ball. Running right, the ball is in his right arm, and running left, the ball is in his left arm.
- Emphasize cutting quickly while moving forward and accelerating to full speed.
- The RB must stay in bounds, drop his shoulder, and rip up through the dummy to score.

Cut and Go

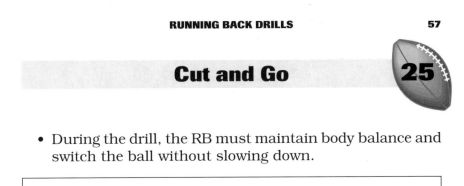

- During the drill, the RB must maintain body balance and switch the ball without slowing down.

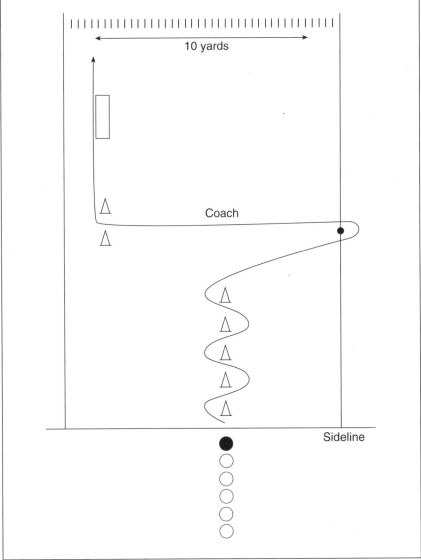

26

Mat Low Block

Coach: Fran Ganter
Team: Penn State
Head Coach: Joe Paterno

Purpose: To teach and practice the proper fundamentals of the low block.

Procedure:

1. Place a portable scrimmage line guide on the ground with a tall, round, stand-up dummy on the defensive side of the line of scrimmage, corresponding to a normal DE or LB alignment.
2. Place a four- by six-foot (or larger) soft mat four yards directly behind the dummy.
3. The RB assumes his normal backfield alignment.
4. On signal, the RB attacks and executes a low block on the dummy, following through properly so that he lands belly down on the mat.

Key Points:

- Emphasize the importance of exploding out of the stance with a straight line angle of attack.
- Remind the blocker to overcome the shock of impact.
- Immediately before contact, the RB must plant and drive upfield, making contact with his inside shoulder on the outside thigh guard of the defender.
- Upon contact, the RB accelerates through the block with his head and eyes up, both feet on the ground.
- The mat placed four yards behind the dummy makes the RB run through the block.
- By standing on the back edge of the mat, the coach can evaluate attack angle, striking points, head position, and follow-through.

Mat Low Block

26

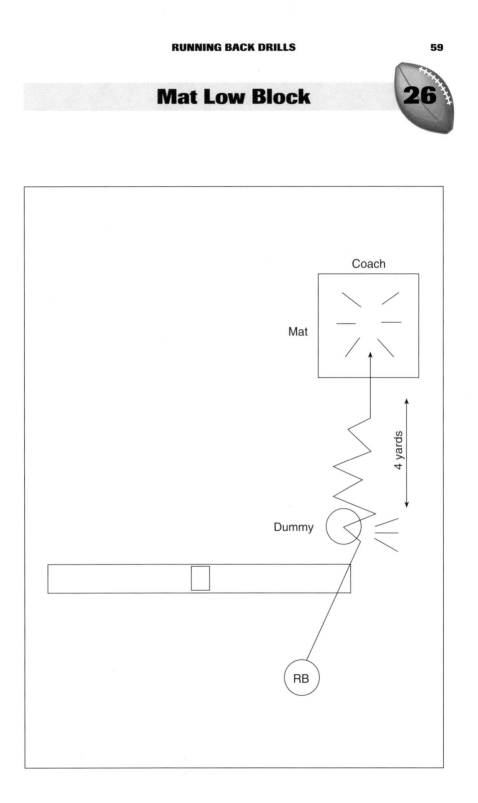

Da Bone

Coach: Walt Hunt
Team: University of Puget Sound
Head Coach: Gordon Elliott

Purpose: To teach hand and arm techniques to RBs.

Procedure:

1. RBs pair up. One RB is on his knees, six inches away from a stand-up bag held by the other.

2. In sequence, teach the following RB techniques:

   a. "Da Bone" (flipper): Bring forearms up forcefully.

   b. Two-hand open jam: Bring arms up fixed, with open palms and cocked wrists.

   c. Rip: Bring arm across body to strike outside portion of defender.

   d. "Tyson": Bring open hand up quickly to strike and escape.

   e. "Heisman": Fully extend arms to keep defender away.

3. On the whistle, RB from an upright body position recoils to strike the blow.

Key Points:

- In the flipper, the RB brings his arms up from belt high to a fixed 90-degree position to strike through the defender at pectoral height. Use this technique against LBs (ISO), when running through a defender, or when power blocking.

- In the two-hand open jam, the RB brings his arms up from belt high with open hands and cocked wrists to strike the defender at pectoral height. The RB then recoils to prevent the defender from grabbing his arms and pulling him down. Use this technique in pass protection.

- In the rip, the RB brings his arm, fixed at a 90-degree angle, up from his hips to strike the outside portion of the defender. Use this technique to avoid a tackle and escape a defender.

Da Bone

- In the "Tyson," the target for a quick blow is the defender's upper arms.
- Use the "Heisman" (stiff arm) in the open field.
- Enhance the drill by doing repetitions with either arm and combinations, by stepping back, or by varying starting position while moving the bag laterally or horizontally.

28 Hand Down Bag

Coach: Jud Keim
Team: California Lutheran University
Head Coach: Scott Squires

Purpose: To teach RBs how to maintain proper body control while running with the football.

Procedure:
1. Divide the players into two single file lines, facing the same direction, 5 yards apart.
2. Each line has two footballs. The first ball carrier in each line holds a ball in his right arm (emphasize ball security).
3. The drill begins when the ball carrier runs forward to touch his off hand on the ground four times in 15 yards. After two or three repetitions, the ball carrier switches arms.
4. Stand between the lines holding a bag. Slam the bag into the legs of the ball carrier two or three times.

Key Points:
- Insist that the ball carrier recover from an off-balance position with good technique, which involves good leg drive with the back, hips, and shoulders up and forward.
- Encourage the ball carrier to maintain his balance by picking up his feet.
- Try to knock the ball carrier off-balance with the bag at the same time he puts his off hand on the ground.
- Emphasize ball security throughout the drill.

Hand Down Bag

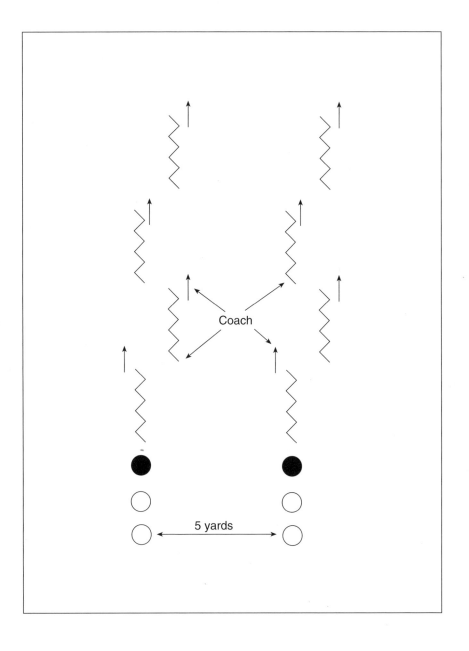

Coach

5 yards

29   **Blast**

Coach: Kelly Skipper
Team: Fresno State
Head Coach: Pat Hill

Purpose: To teach RBs to explode to the point of attack and run through defenders.

Procedure:

1. Place four dummy bags on the ground in a row, three yards apart.
2. Four yards in front of the first bag, two players hold stand-up (push) bags.
3. The ball carrier (without the ball) aligns off to the side of the stand-up bags, ready to receive a handoff from the QB.
4. Stand three yards away from the fourth dummy bag, ready to signal a directional cut to the ball carrier.
5. The drill starts when the QB reverse pivots and hands off to the ball carrier.
6. The ball carrier blasts through the push bags, steps over each dummy bag, and executes a right or left cut.

Key Points:

- The ball carrier must explode though the line of scrimmage after receiving the handoff.
- The ball carrier must use high knee action throughout the drill.
- Emphasize that the ball carrier's shoulder must lean forward to gain momentum.
- After exiting the bags, the ball carrier keys on the coach's signal to make his cut.
- Always have the ball carrier tuck the ball away.
- Conduct this drill at full speed and in both directions.

Blast

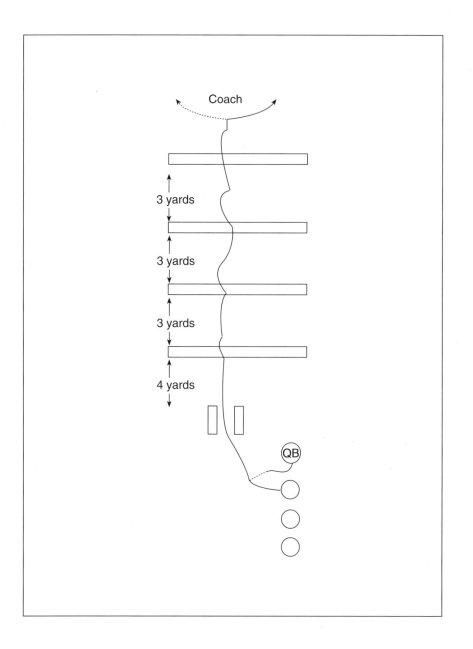

Hide-and-Seek

Coach: Don Treadwell
Team: Stanford University
Head Coach: Tyrone Willingham

Purpose: To practice agility and coming back to catch the ball after finding the lane in which the QB can throw.

Procedure:

1. Use as many large bags as desired, depending on the available teaching station.
2. The RBs align in a single file next to the first bag. On command, the first RB shuffles behind and tightly around the bag.
3. QBs (or coaches) align in front of each bag, and toss the ball to each RB as he comes out from behind the bag.
4. The next RB in line begins after the player ahead of him catches the ball and tosses it back to the thrower.
5. Players continue this sequence in one direction until all RBs are finished.

Key Points:

- The RBs must round the bag tightly to force an obvious lane for QB to throw the ball.
- Throw the ball when the RB is behind the bag, so that he finds it when he comes back around the bag.
- The RB must keep his feet moving during the entire drill.
- Run this drill in both directions. It is excellent for simulating short dump-off type routes.

Hide-and-Seek

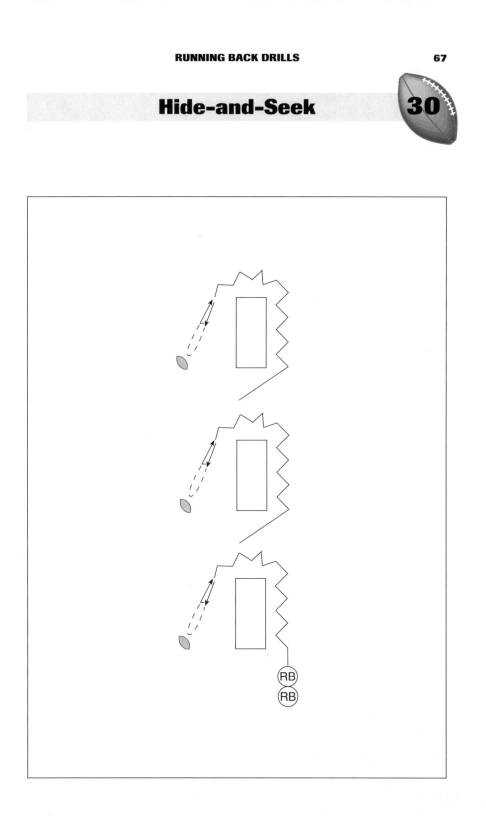

Blitz Pickup

Coach: Bob Visger
Team: California State University at Sacramento
Head Coach: John Volek

Purpose: To teach backs to read and block defensive blitzes and twists.

Procedure:

1. Place six large trash cans on the line of scrimmage to represent an offensive line (including the tight end).
2. Align three LBs behind the trash cans, ready to run through them.
3. Align the RB in a called set. He must be prepared to carry out his protection assignment.
4. Stand behind the RB:

    a. Designate stunts for the LBs by holding up cards.

    b. Give the offensive play to the RB with a cadence call.
5. On the starting count, LBs run stunts and the RB executes his assigned block.

Key Points:

- The RB must start in correct stance, know the protection schemes used by the line and tight ends, and execute the correct assignment.
- Emphasize the RB's ability to recognize his assignment.

    a. Dual read: inside LB to outside LB.

    b. Far read: perimeter to inside LB.
- The RB must clear the QB (drop steps) and get to his blocking area quickly.
- During the drill, the RB must be aware of audibles which may change his assignment.
- The RB must execute proper pass protection techniques.
- Variation: Some calls might require the RB to run a short pass route or replace the tight end.

Blitz Pickup

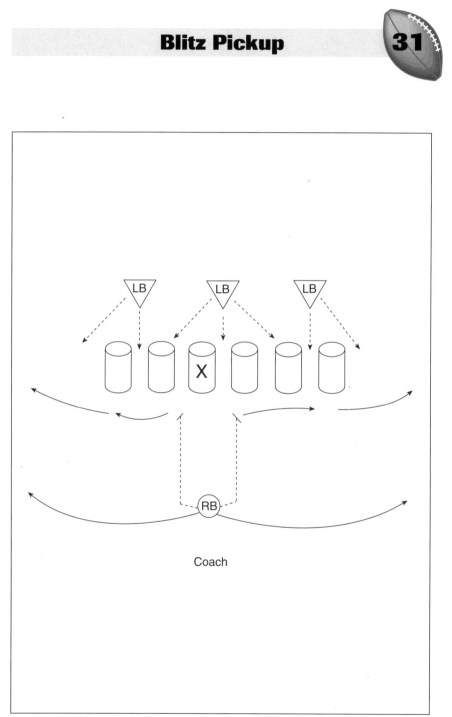

Coach

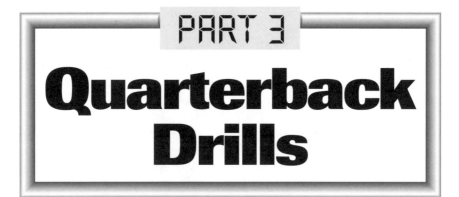

PART 3

Quarterback Drills

The quarterback gets all the glory—or all the grief. Because they perform in the spotlight, quarterbacks must have enough confidence to handle criticism and still be able to lead and enough humility to credit the teammates who help them succeed.

A quarterback must have a special combination of mental and physical skills. Roger Staubach, Fran Tarkenton, Joe Montana, and Charlie Ward used their intelligence and quick feet to get their teams into the end zone, even on plays that appeared to be dead ends. Dan Marino, John Elway, and Brett Favre employ their field generalship and rifle-like arms to shoot bull's-eyes through and over the defense. Great quarterbacks possess a unique mind-body makeup that allows them to see the entire field, feel defensive pressure, make split-second decisions, and execute with precision. The drills in this section of the book will help develop your quarterback's mental and physical tools.

It's no surprise that programs that have historically emphasized the passing game, such as Brigham Young (Gifford Nielsen, Jim McMahon, Steve Young, Ty Detmer) and Stanford (John Brodie, Jim Plunkett, John Elway), have produced some of the game's most prolific quarterbacks. In today's game, programs at all levels are developing excellent quarterbacks using all types of offensive attacks. Now let's see what drills some of the best quarterback coaches use to set the stage for success at this key position.

Quarterback Drills

Drill	Coach	Team
32 QB—Hokie Style	Rickey Bustle	Virginia Tech
33 Slide	Bill Diedrick	Washington
34 Quick Release	Ray Dorr	Texas A&M
35 QB's Drop Breakdown	Mike Dunbar	Northern Iowa
36 Quarterback Resets	Steve Fairchild	Colorado State
37 Point-to-Point	Steve Hagen	San Jose State
38 Read	Leon Hart	Eastern Kentucky
39 Quarterback Drop, Pressure, and Reset	Woody McCorvey	Alabama
40 Shuffle	Tom O'Brien	Boston College
41 Line	Sean Payton	Philadelphia Eagles
42 Bootleg Pass	George Perry	Cheyenne H.S. (NV)
43 Angle Throw	Mark Richt	Florida State
44 Net Control	Eddie Robinson, Jr.	Grambling State
45 Option Keep or Pitch	Homer Smith	Arizona
46 Pocket Movement	Roger Theder	Formerly with San Jose State
47 Flash	Jeff Zenisek	Northern Iowa

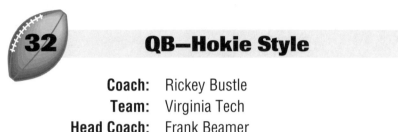

32   QB—Hokie Style

Coach: Rickey Bustle
Team: Virginia Tech
Head Coach: Frank Beamer

Purpose: To teach and practice the proper execution of the pass set and delivery.

Procedure:

1. Align three QBs (with the ball) with their toes on a yard line and three QBs on the opposite hashmark, 10 yards apart.

2. In sequence, teach the following QB techniques:

   a. Three-step pass set

   b. Five-step pass set

   c. Sprintout

   d. Sprint draw

3. On command, three QBs execute the called technique and each throws crossfield to another QB.

Key Points:

- The QB must dig his opposite toe into the turf, bring the ball to his chest, let his arms work natually, and explode either two or three steps off the line of scrimmage.

  a. Take a deep first step, past six o'clock, for all four techniques.

  b. In the three-step drop, take the second and third steps straight back with the third step shorter. On the third step, the QB pivots and releases the ball.

  c. In the five-step drop, take the second and later steps straight back with the fifth step shorter. On the fifth step, the QB bounces up on his toes, pivots, and releases the ball.

  d. In the sprintout, the second and third steps are slightly flattened deep crossovers, the third step slightly deeper. The QB then sprints on an arch six and a half yards

QB—Hokie Style

deep, gets his shoulders square to the target, and releases the ball.

e. In the sprint draw, the second step is a deep crossover. The third and fourth steps are straight back. The QB then fakes a draw, comes straight back off the fake, bounces up on his toes, pivots, and releases the ball.

- After five throws back and forth, QBs switch hashmarks and repeat the drill.

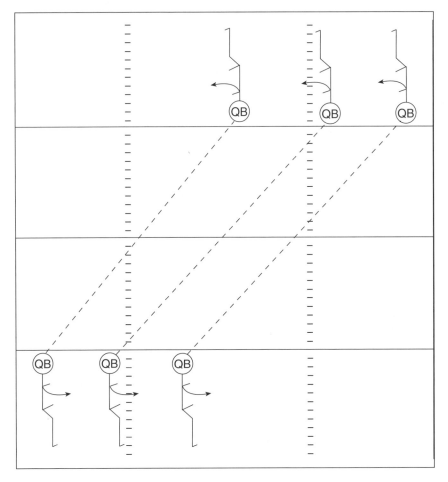

33   Slide

Coach: Bill Diedrick
Team: University of Washington
Head Coach: Jim Lambright

Purpose: To train the QB how to avoid defensive pressure in the pocket.

Procedure:
1. The QB (with the ball) faces a stationary receiver who is 10 yards downfield, directly across from the ball.
2. A DE or coach aligns on the line of scrimmage for an outside rush on the QB.
3. To begin the drill, the QB executes a five-step drop. The rusher comes toward the QB from the QB's right or left side.
4. The QB feels the pressure and slides away to step back into the pocket.
5. In the pocket, the QB resets his feet, takes a step, and throws the ball to the receiver.

Key Points:
- Ensure that the QB keeps his eyes downfield.
- The QB must be set before executing the slide technique.
- The rusher must get his hands up to put pressure on the QB.
- The QB must step back in the pocket, reset his feet, and step toward the receiver while throwing.
- This is an excellant drill for training the QB to avoid pressure.
- Work the drill so pressure comes from both sides.

Slide

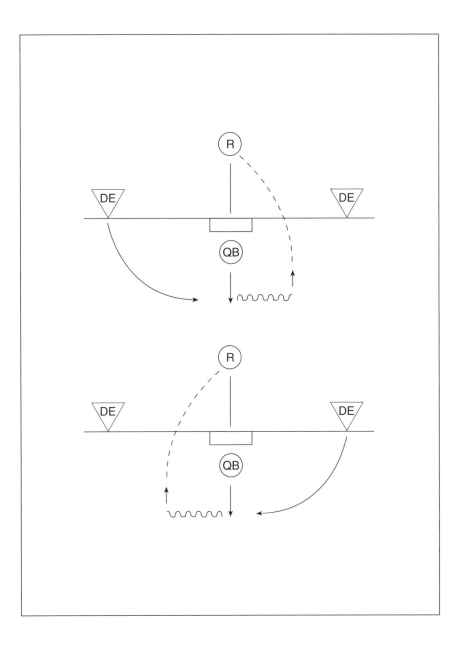

34   Quick Release

Coach: Ray Dorr
Team: Texas A&M University
Head Coach: R.C. Slocum

Purpose: To develop the QB's quick release upon defensive movement.

Procedure:

1. Align two receivers, 17 yards downfield and 12 yards apart, facing the QB.
2. Align two defenders, 14 yards downfield in the middle between the two receivers, one behind the other.
3. The QB (with the ball) begins the drill by shuffling forward to a line one yard in front of his feet.
4. The front defender breaks either direction laterally when the QB's front foot touches the line.
5. The secondary defender keys the back of front defender, then reacts by moving laterally in the opposite direction.
6. The QB releases the football opposite the front defender's lateral movement to a stationary receiver (if the front defender moves to the QB's right, he throws left).

Key Points:

- Both defenders must break laterally, but in opposite directions.
- The QB's visual reaction to the front defender will improve the QB's concentration and field vision.
- The QB's concentration and anticipation helps to develop his quick release.
- This drill is very competitive, placing a high premium on throwing away from defenders.
- Stress ball velocity.

Quick Release

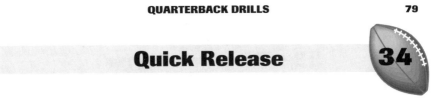

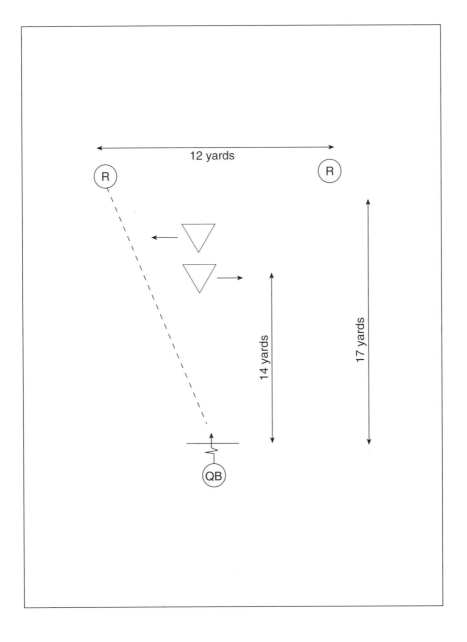

35   QB's Drop Breakdown

Coach: Mike Dunbar
Team: Northern Iowa
Head Coach: Mike Dunbar

Purpose: To break down each step of the QB's drop technique.

Procedure:

1. Set QBs behind OCs (with the ball), five yards apart, on the sideline facing you.
2. Stand off the field and call out the steps.
3. The QB takes a staggered stance and before the snap transfers his weight mentally to the instep of the opposite (back) foot.
4. On the first step, an open reach, the QB sits down as he push-pivots, leaning for speed.
5. On the second step, the QB combines the first step with a speed crossover, down the midline (straight back), bringing the ball into a ready position.
6. On the third step, the QB drives his knee for depth.
7. The QB takes a smaller fourth step in stride, standing more erect to gain balance.
8. On the fifth step, QB changes direction by putting his weight on the balls of his feet, which should be hip-width apart.

Key Points:

- Drill and explain each individual step and combinations of steps.
- When executing the crossover step, swing the ball like a pendulum, armpit to armpit at chest level, for speed and balance.
- Teach the QB to lean for speed and really stretch the groin in his drop steps.
- The key to a five-step drop is the third step in which the QB must feel the burst for depth.

QB's Drop Breakdown 35

- On the snap, emphasize the QB's ability to separate from the OC with speed and depth and vision of the entire field.
- On the fourth step, the QB should land flat-footed to reduce and redirect momentum while feeling the weight transfer of his upper body.
- At the end of the drop, the QB "frames up" by getting his feet, hip, shoulder, and head pointed in the direction he is going to throw.

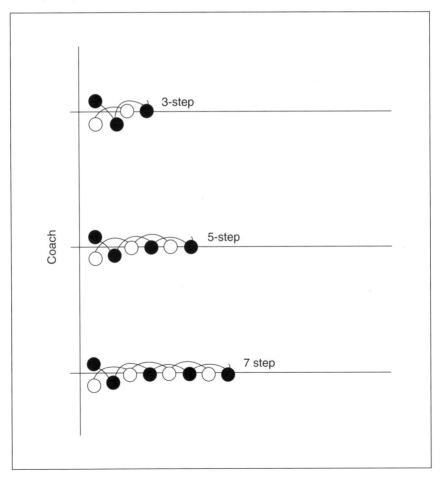

36 Quarterback Resets

Coach: Steve Fairchild
Team: Colorado State University
Head Coach: Sonny Lubick

Purpose: To teach the QB how to shuffle and make an accurate throw after setting up in the pocket.

Procedure:

1. Position a receiver 15 to 20 yards upfield as a target for the QB.
2. The coach stands 2 to 3 yards in front of the QB's proper set-up position, slightly to one side (out of the drop path).
3. To begin the drill, the QB must start from a proper stance.
4. The QB takes the snap from the OC and executes a three-, five-, or seven-step drop.
5. The coach steps toward the QB after he sets up in the pocket.
6. The QB moves to his right or left, or steps forward, away from coach's movement.
7. After shuffling to reset his feet, the QB throws to the target.

Key Points:

- The QB holds the ball in both hands and maintains eye contact with the target throughout the drill.
- While using the shuffle technique, the QB must take short steps and maintain a narrow base.
- The QB's front shoulder should not rise up while throwing.
- Make this drill part of every offensive practice.

Quarterback Resets

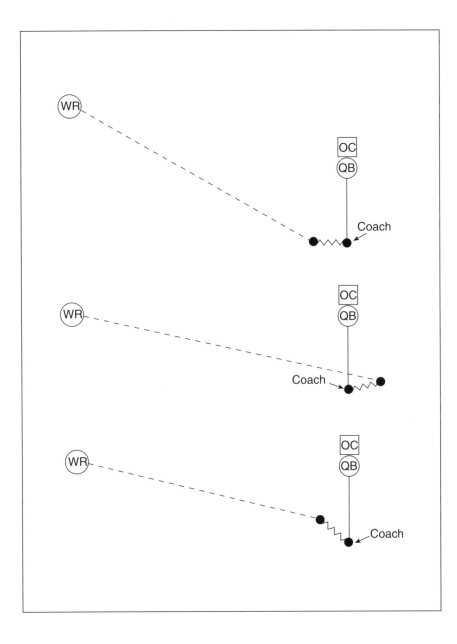

37   # **Point-to-Point**

Coach: Steve Hagen
Team: San Jose State
Head Coach: Dave Baldwin

Purpose: To teach proper throwing mechanics to improve passing accuracy.

Procedure:

1. Two QBs stand 15 yards apart, playing catch with each other.
2. The object is throw the ball so that the lead point hits the QB (receiver) on the point of his nose.
3. The coach aligns in position to teach and correct the delivery of the ball by each QB.

Key Points:

- Emphasize these fundamentals to teach and practice proper throwing technique:

    a. The QB must cup the ball, pointing the lead point of the ball at the target.

    b. The QB's shoulders start perpendicular to the line of scrimmage and complete a full rotation upon release of the ball.

    c. The QB's throwing elbow must be parallel to the shoulder but no higher than the ear.

- After the release, if the ball tails or dies, teach the QB to bring the lead point around toward the target more to create a better spiral.

Point-to-Point

38   Read

Coach: Leon Hart
Team: Eastern Kentucky University
Head Coach: Roy Kidd

Purpose: To train the QB to read different coverages and deliver the ball on time to the open receiver.

Procedure:

1. Align the WR, TE, RBs, and QB in the desired formation with a secondary and LBs aligned opposite them.
2. From behind the offensive team, the coach calls out the desired routes and which side of the drill is live. The offense lines up in formation, and the coach uses finger signals or signs to tell the defense the coverage and desired action.
3. The QB calls cadence, takes the snap from the OC or snapping machine, and drops back while live receivers and backs run the called routes against the assigned defensive coverage.
4. The QB reads the coverage, then throws the ball on time to the open receiver.
5. The alternate QB repeats the same play to the other side, which is now live. The coach may choose to give a new call, cadence, and coverage.

Key Points:

- In this controlled setting, the coach can simulate a variety of coverages and looks for the QB and receivers.
- By standing behind the offense, the coach can see whether the receivers are running the correct routes against the coverage.
- By standing behind the offense, the coach can see whether the QB takes his proper depth, correctly reads the coverage stimulus, and throws to the open receiver.
- Players assigned defensive drops or movement (e.g., blitz) must go full speed, moving quickly from one live side to

Read

another. This allows everyone to get enough reps in a short period of time.

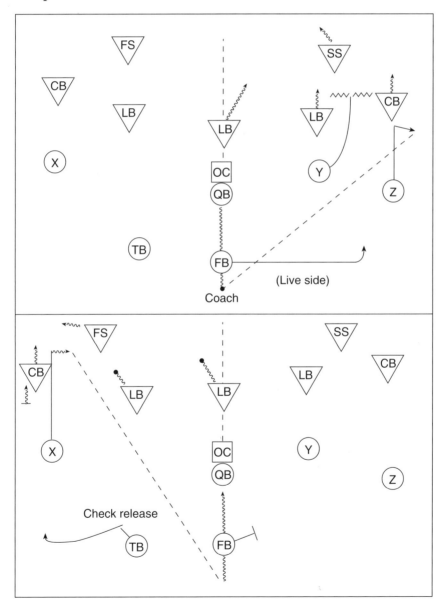

39   **Quarterback Drop, Pressure, and Reset**

Coach: Woody McCorvey
Team: University of Alabama
Head Coach: Mike DuBose

Purpose: To train the QB to make a proper drop, develop pocket awareness, feel pressure, and reset his feet.

Procedure:

1. Space two dummies seven yards apart, with their backs facing inside at a 45-degree angle.
2. A defender aligns in front of each bag at the line of scrimmage and rushes the QB on ball movement.
3. The QB takes the ball from the OC on a snap count and executes a five-step drop.
4. To pressure *inside*, the rusher delays one second, makes an outside move, takes the rushing lane inside the dummy, and runs at 3/4 speed toward the QB.
5. To pressure *outside*, the rusher delays one second, makes an inside move, takes the lane outside the dummy, and runs by the QB at 3/4 speed.
6. On command, the QB resets, pulls down the ball, and runs.

Key Points:

- Always give the QB a pattern that fits your system. He must look downfield where the pattern is developing.
- Alternate right and left inside pressure.
- On inside pressure, the QB steps toward and around the rush, then resets his feet in preparation for throwing downfield as the pattern develops.
- On outside pressure, the QB steps up into the pocket and resets his feet in preparation for throwing downfield as the pattern develops.
- On outside pressure, the QB should see the rush coming as well as feel pressure from the backside.

Quarterback Drop, Pressure, and Reset

- To execute the outside pressure after alternating, the rush should come from both sides simultaneously, which gives the QB a true picture.

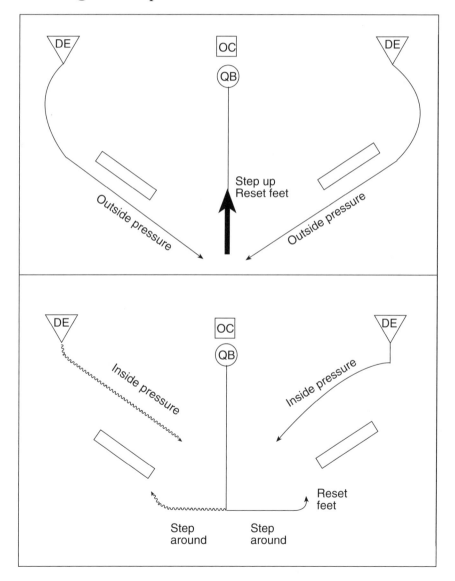

40   Shuffle

Coach: Tom O'Brien
Team: Boston College
Head Coach: Tom O'Brien

Purpose: To teach the QB proper technique for avoiding the pass rush and for resetting his feet to make a good throw to the outlet receiver.

Procedure:

1. The QB takes a snap from the coach, then takes a five-step drop.
2. Align two other QBs on the line of scrimmage to rush the passer in predetermined lanes with a receiver nearby.
3. The rushers wait to move until the QB gets behind them.
4. The QB sets his feet in the pocket. He then shuffles to his right or left or avoids the rush by stepping up in the pocket.
5. After shuffling, the QB resets his feet, then throws to an outlet receiver.

Key Points:

- Keep a close check on the QB's initial set-up.
- Stress ball security while the QB moves to avoid the rush.
- Observe the QB very closely for proper technique, especially when he is resetting his feet.
- Rotate the QBs. Those assigned to rush must work hard to put pressure on the drop-back QB.
- You can designate different outlet receivers and ask the QB to find them while being rushed.

Shuffle

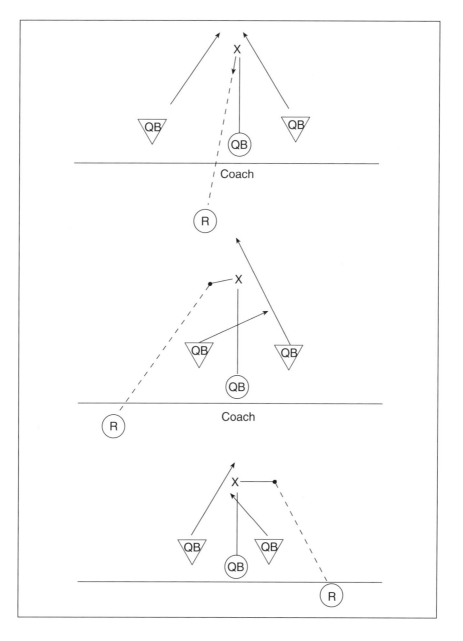

41 Line

Coach: Sean Payton
Team: Philadelphia Eagles
Head Coach: Ray Rhodes

Purpose: To develop the QB's mechanics for throwing the ball on the run.

Procedure:

1. Align QBs on the sideline, 10 yards apart.
2. Two QBs face off against each other with one football.
3. The QB without the ball aligns 5 yards forward on his yard line.
4. The QBs start throwing the ball to one another while running crossfield.
5. When they past the first hashmark, the second pair of QBs begins to throw, and both pairs finish at the opposite sideline.
6. All QBs return to the original sideline by repeating the drill.

Key Points:

- The receiving QB always hustles ahead to stagger himself for the reception.
- Vary the depth between the QBs to simulate particular routes within the offense.
- The QBs must work toward the target, not throw across their bodies.
- Coach the QBs to maintain proper balance as they turn and get ready to throw by taking smaller steps.
- Emphasize that the QB point his off shoulder at the target (left shoulder for right-hand throwers, right shoulder for left-hand throwers).
- This drill is especially good for improving sprintouts, rollouts, and bootlegs.

Line

41

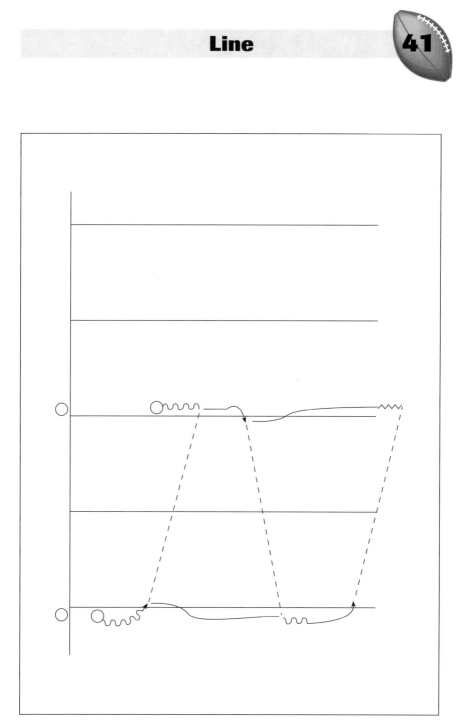

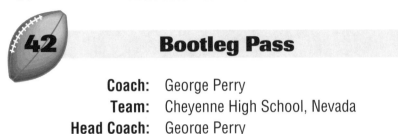

Bootleg Pass

Coach: George Perry
Team: Cheyenne High School, Nevada
Head Coach: George Perry

Purpose: To teach the QB to read the routes of receivers while executing the bootleg pass with proper footwork.

Procedure:

1. The QB takes a snap from the OC, runs a buck sweep right, fakes a handoff to both the FB and TB, and then bootlegs to the left.

2. After the fake, the FB releases into the weakside flat as a receiver (#2), and the TB blocks the strongside DE.

3. The SE (#1) runs an 18-yard comeback route, the TE (#3) runs an 8- to 10-yard crossing route, and the WB (#4) runs a deep post route.

4. As the coach calls out a number, the QB uses proper footwork to throw to the called receiver.

Key Points:

- Stand behind the QB so you can observe and correct the QB's footwork.
- Run this drill in both directions.
- Alternate the drill by having the QB throw in progression.
- Don't allow the QB to anticipate the number you call.

Bootleg Pass

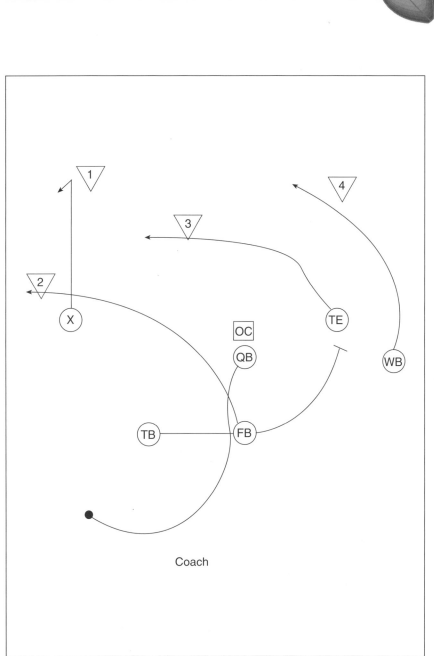

43 **Angle Throw**

Coach: Mark Richt
Team: Florida State University
Head Coach: Bobby Bowden

Purpose: To prepare the QB to throw three-, five-, or seven-step drop passes.

Procedure:

1. QBs pair up, each one on a hashmark.
2. To execute the three-, five- or seven-step drop, one QB (with the ball) aligns 1.5 yards off the line of scrimmage. The other QB (receiver) aligns downfield to catch the ball.
3. The QB throws a stop route to the receiver:
   a. Throw to the receiver 6 yards upfield from a three-step drop.
   b. Throw to the receiver 10 to 12 yards upfield from a five-step drop.
   c. Throw to the receiver 16 to 18 yards upfield from a seven-step drop.
4. After four throws back and forth, QBs switch hashmarks to repeat the drill.

Key Points:

- Each QB must warm up properly before beginning the drill.
- Ensure that all QBs have previously practiced the proper execution of each drop set.
- The receiving QB's feet must be at the proper depth for the designated route.
- To simulate a snap, the QB puts the ball in his nonthrowing hand and upon cadence will pop it into his throwing hand.
- Expand this drill by having additional QBs work in tandem off the other QBs. Keep the same cadence.

Angle Throw

43

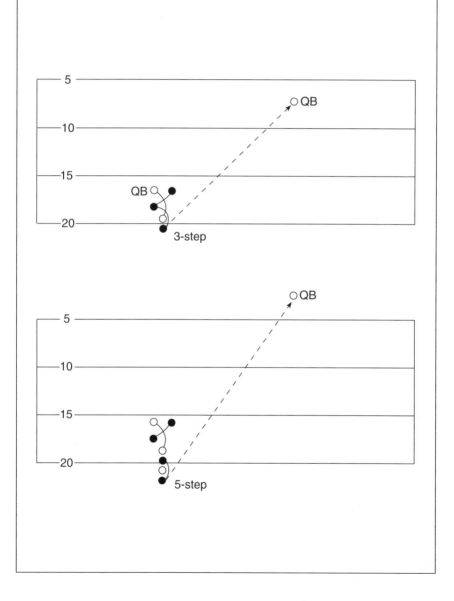

Net Control

Coach: Eddie Robinson, Jr.
Team: Grambling State University
Head Coach: Eddie Robinson, Sr.

Purpose: To improve the QB's throwing mechanics, steps, body position, progression reads, and accuracy.

Procedure:

1. Place two stand-up nets, representing X and Z, 12 to 14 yards downfield near the hashmarks. Place a third stand-up net, representing Y, 8 to 10 yards downfield over center. Place two more stand-up nets, representing HB or TB and FB, flared 8 to 10 yards wide.

2. On the snap count, the QB begins a back-pedal drop by first stepping back with the foot on the same side as his throwing arm.

3. The QB drops back five steps, stops, and throws into the Y net.

4. The QB immediately returns to take another snap. This time he drops back five steps, stops, looks at the Y net, pauses, and repositions himself, then throws into the Z net.

5. The QB again returns to take another snap. This time he drops back five steps, next looks and pauses at both Y and Z, then repositions himself and throws into the HB or TB net.

6. Repeat steps 3 through 5, this time progressing from Y to X to FB.

7. The drill ends after each QB has thrown three times each to his right and left.

Key Points:

- The nets represent a control pass. The QB's progression for this drill is as follows:

  a. Y on an 8-yard middle curl

Net Control

b. Z or X on a 12- to 14-yard curl

c. RB running a moderate speed flare route

- Monitor the QB's steps and body positioning so that he can step toward and throw with accuracy into the square net built in the upper part of the standing net.

- Look for and correct any mistake made by the QB in going through the progression.

- Grambling uses the back-pedal drop technique because it gives the QB a greater range of vision.

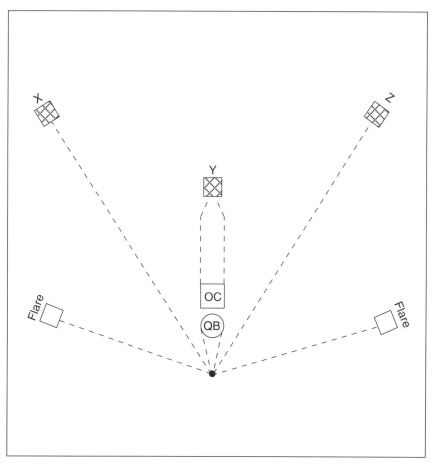

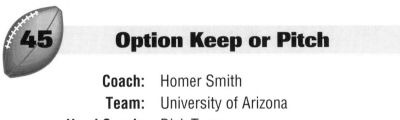

45   Option Keep or Pitch

Coach: Homer Smith
Team: University of Arizona
Head Coach: Dick Tomey

Purpose: To train the option QB to correctly decide to either keep or pitch.

Procedure:

1. The teaching station includes four participants (all QBs), who are numbered 1 (QB), 2 (LB), 3 (end-of-line defender), and 4 (RB to receive pitch).
2. Position yourself in the same place whether the play runs to the right or the left.
3. Each player rotates clockwise by number after running the option twice to each side.
4. This drill uses seven different defensive schemes to test the QB's reads (a-g).
5. To complete the drill, add two more players. One blocks the DE, and the other is defensive support on the perimeter. For alignment see diagrams h and i.

Drill Options:

- Diagram a: The DE runs straight at the QB. Teach the QB to stop himself with his heel cleats, delay until the RB gets to a 45-degree angle from LOS, and then pitch.
- Diagram b: The DE comes across too deep. If the DE goes for the QB's hand, the QB executes the pitch. If the pitch is denied, QB keeps upfield.
- Diagram c: The DE backs away from the QB. The QB accelerates at the shoulder of DE to pitch or reacts to danger and keeps.
- Diagram d: The DE penetrates inside the coach. The QB knows not to pitch off the DT, so he reacts to the interruption and keeps.

Option Keep or Pitch 45

- Diagram e: When the pitchman is not in the QB's periph- eral vision, the QB simulates a mistake and keeps.

- Diagram f: When the DE disappears, the QB turns his shoulder to the replacement inside defender and pitches.

- Diagram g: When the DE crosses with an outside defender, the QB fakes the pitch and keeps upfield for the first down.

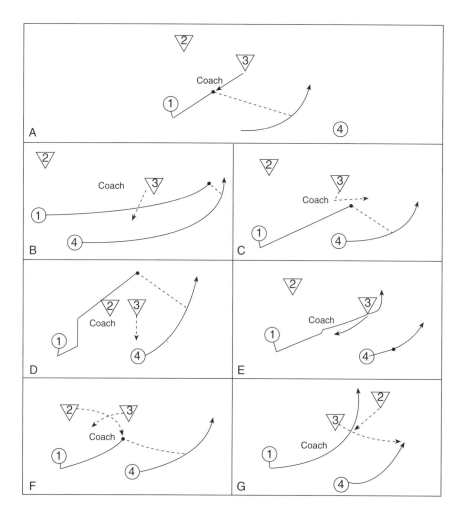

46   Pocket Movement

Coach: Roger Theder
Team: Formerly with San Jose State

Purpose: To teach the QB to focus on his receiver while avoiding the rush in the pocket.

Procedure:

1. While focusing on the target, the QB (with the ball) takes either a five- or seven-step drop with a coach or another QB acting as pass rusher.
2. The rusher uses either an inside or outside rush to get to the QB.
3. To avoid the inside rush, the QB uses the slide technique, then throws.
4. To avoid the outside rush, the QB steps up, then throws.
5. Coach may vary the depth of the receiver.

Key Points:

- When the QB sees the receiver snap up, he should be ready to release the ball at any time.
- Emphasize that the QB must keep both hands on the ball until ready to release.
- The QB must keep a rhythm and maintain his hip and shoulder direction while practicing his quick release.
- Good throwing technique requires the QB to snap his nonthrowing hand through, keep his chin down, and bring his back shoulder up.
- Executing this drill properly calls for timing and accuracy.

Pocket Movement

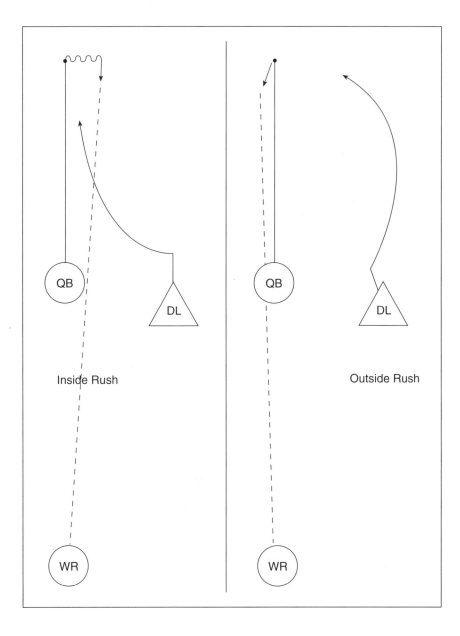

Inside Rush

Outside Rush

Flash

Coach: Jeff Zenisek
Team: Northern Iowa University
Head Coach: Mike Dunbar

Purpose: To train the QB to read an open receiver within an area.

Procedure:

1. Three receivers align 8 to 14 yards deep, 5 yards apart.
2. The QB (with the ball) takes either a three-step or five-step drop.
3. Standing behind the QB, the coach signals to one of the receivers to flash his hands.
4. The QB steps, then throws immediately to the flashed hands.

Key Points:

- To be successful in this drill, the QB must keep his eyes on the area, not on a particular receiver, while using his head as a swivel.
- The QB must keep his feet moving while setting up in the pocket.
- While in the pocket, the QB must keep the ball in high shoulder position.
- This drill helps the QB practice moving his feet beneath his shoulder pads and stepping toward the target.
- Variation: Add additional receivers to the right or left in order to work on the bootleg, rollout, or sprintout.

Flash

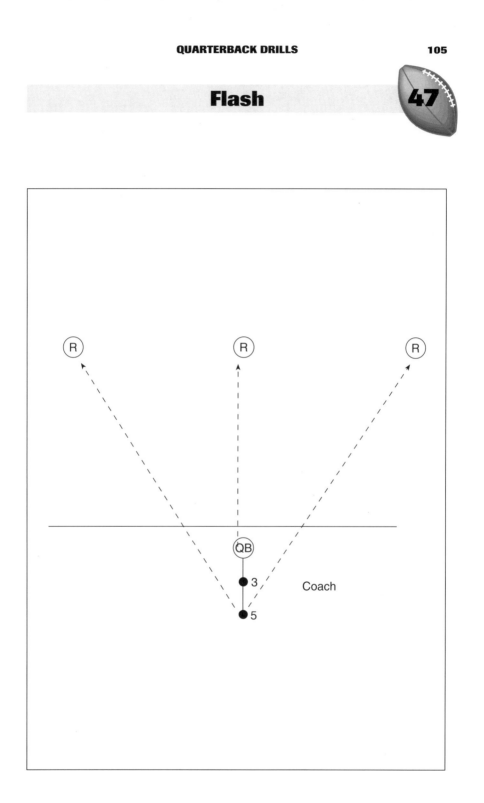

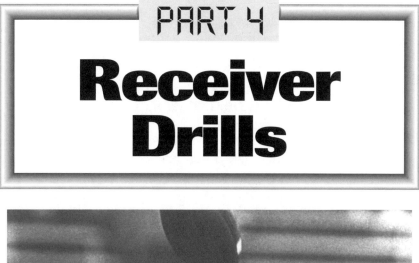

PART 4

Receiver Drills

Receiver positions include split end or wide receiver, flanker, and tight end. Traditional "Xs and Os" terminology calls positions X, Z, and Y, respectively.

Wide receivers and flankers tend to have similar physical attributes—speed, agility, jumping ability, and "soft" hands. However, wide-outs are often a bit faster, presenting a breakaway threat, while flankers typically pack a few more pounds to help them block downfield and catch the ball in traffic.

Tight ends are now almost as large as offensive tackles, yet nearly as fast as many flankers. Because a tight end is a blocker and a receiver, he must have both enough strength and size to block defensive linemen and enough speed to get downfield and open on pass plays. Because of their dual responsibilities of blocking and receiving, tight ends drill with the offensive linemen as much as they do with the receiving corps. This typically gives tight ends a toughness that's hard to miss. Guys like John Mackey, Jackie Smith, Mike Ditka, Russ Francis, and Kellen Winslow happily run over or by defenders.

Although history's greatest wide receivers and flankers, such as Jerry Rice, Charlie Joiner, Raymond Berry, Paul Warfield, Charley Taylor, Steve Largent, Fred Biletnikoff, Don Hutson, and Lance Alworth, differed considerably in style, they all did one thing exceptionally well: Catch the football. Receivers like these men make an average quarterback good and a good quarterback great.

The drills in this chapter will help receivers develop the toughness and technique to be their best at the position. Don't drop the ball—run them regularly and put more production into your passing attack.

Receiver Drills

Drill		Coach	Team
48	Tight End Four-in-One	Dick Arbuckle	Arizona State
49	Running Post Routes Against Man Coverage	Tommy Bowden	Tulane
50	Distraction	Gregg Brandon	Northwestern University
51	Lamborghini	Tim Brewster	North Carolina
52	Curl	Bill Cockhill	Montana
53	Fly-By	Kevin Faulkner	New Mexico
54	Pass Line	Martin Fine	Indiana
55	Great Catch	Mike Garrison	Kansas
56	Pass Gauntlet	Greg Gatlin	College of Siskiyous (CA)
57	Vision	Dirk Koetter	Oregon
58	Fit-Ladder	Mike Mahoney	St. Lawrence University
59	Top End With Collision	Urban Meyer	Notre Dame
60	Distraction	Kirk Parrish	Texas A&M
61	Towel	Don Patterson	Iowa
62	Cones—Burst	John Shannon	Jackson State
63	The Square	Pat Shurmur	Michigan State

48   Tight End Four-in-One

Coach: Dick Arbuckle
Team: Arizona State University
Head Coach: Bruce Snyder

Purpose: To improve all phases of the pass route for TEs.

Procedure:

1. Place three stand-up bags as follows: (1) in front of the TE, (2) 10 yards downfield, and (3) 5 yards further downfield at an angle from second bag.
2. Place one hand shield 10 yards horizontally from the third bag.
3. On the line of scrimmage, align the QB with the OC for the snap and the TE directly in front of bag #1.
4. On the snap, QB drops to pass. The TE executes his release technique, then runs downfield at bag #2.
5. TE makes a square cut at bag #2, continues across to bag #3, and executes a sift (as against a LB).
6. After the TE clears bag #3, the QB throws to the TE. The TE catches and puts the ball in the far arm.
7. After the catch, TE executes a dip-and-rip technique (as against a DB), then runs upfield.

Key Points:

- Run the drill at 3/4 speed to emphasize proper technique.
- Have the TE vary his release techniques at the line of scrimmage.
- Alternate running the drill between the right and left side of the OC.
- Because this drill concentrates on technique, confine the drill to a limited area.

Tight End Four-in-One

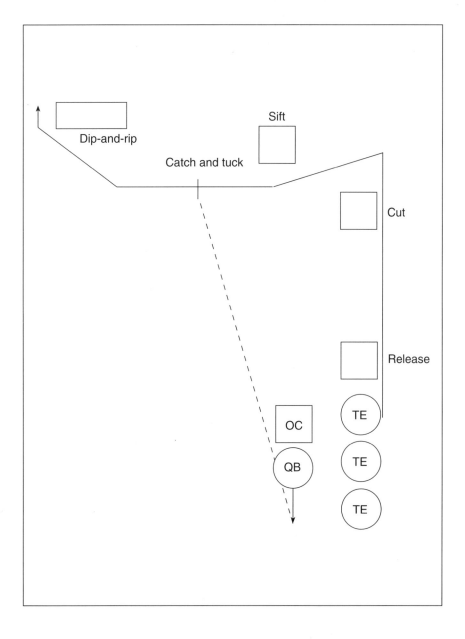

Dip-and-rip

Sift

Catch and tuck

Cut

Release

OC

TE

QB

TE

TE

49 Running Post Routes Against Man Coverage

Coach: Tommy Bowden
Team: Tulane University
Head Coach : Tommy Bowden

Purpose: To have a WR recognize man coverage from a pre-snap read and run a precise post route.

Procedure:

1. DBs align in man coverage look: Safeties show man coverage by lining up closer to the line of scrimmage or offset to one side or both, and the cornerbacks align inside on the WR.

2. To begin the drill, in a pre-snap read both the QB and WR recognize man coverage. This usually indicates a blitz, requiring a quick throw.

3. On the snap, the first step of the WR in running a good post route is to get centered up (head-up) on the CB by pushing inside while pushing upfield at the same time.

4. Once the WR gets head-up on the CB, he sprints to close to within 1 to 2 yards.

5. To execute the post cut, the WR takes a short jab step, simulating a takeoff at his outside shoulder, along with a quick head-and-shoulder fake.

6. The WR continues his post route after the cut as follows:

   a. Against pure man coverage with no middle safety, the post route is away from the CB and slightly crossfield.

   b. Against free man coverage with middle safety, the post route is more upfield, splitting the CB and the S.

   c. Against man coverage when the CB squats at 10 to 12 yards, the post route is over or behind the CB.

Key Points:

• If the WR can't recognize man coverage from the CB alignment, then he must focus on the safety.

Running Post Routes Against Man Coverage

- Any recognition of man coverage from a pre-snap read helps to eliminate false steps.
- The WR must be careful to not make a move more than two yards away from the CB or raise up too high before he runs the post cut.

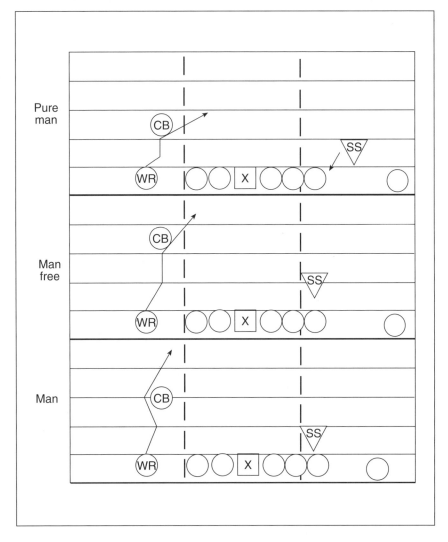

Distraction

Coach: Gregg Brandon
Team: Northwestern University
Head Coach: Gary Barnett

Purpose: To teach receivers to concentrate and catch the ball with defenders moving in front of them.

Procedure:

1. Two stagger lines face each other, 10 yards apart. The front line consists of distracters (defenders), and the back line consists of receivers.

2. Place two cones, 1 yard apart, in front of each line to keep the correct stagger distance.

3. The QB or coach (with the ball) aligns 10 yards from a cone placed downfield at the midpoint line.

4. On the passer's command, the first receiver and first distracter run toward each other.

5. As the two players pass midpoint, the passer throws the ball through the distracter to the receiver.

6. After the catch, the receiver and distracter switch sides.

Key Points:

- Insist that the receiver stay on line and not drift away from the distracter.

- The receiver runs through and catches the ball while on the move.

- During the drill, the distracter must avoid any physical contact with the receiver.

- The drill can be run in both directions.

Distraction

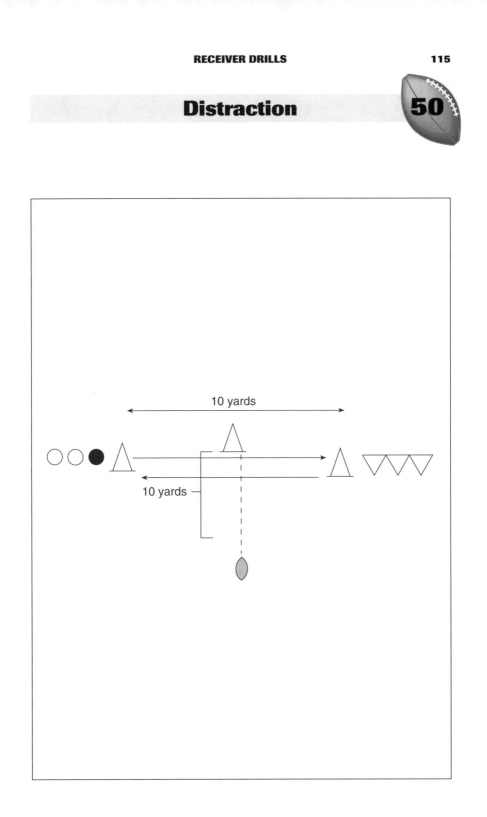

50

51   Lamborghini

Coach: Tim Brewster
Team: University of North Carolina
Head Coach: Mack Brown

Purpose: To teach the TE the proper way to make cuts at optimal speed.

Procedure:

1. Place four cones to form a square, 5 yards on a side.
2. A TE aligns at the first cone, ready to run around the cones.
3. A QB or coach (with the ball) aligns near the fourth cone, ready to throw the ball.
4. On command, the TE makes three speed cuts, then catches the ball coming off the third cone.

Key Points:

- The TE must use the proper foot plant, which is always the outside foot, whether going left or right.
- Emphasize speed, acceleration out of each cut, and running like a sprinter (hands high and weight down) throughout the drill.
- Coach the TE to maintain proper body position at the break point, which is weight over the toes and heels off the ground.
- To square the shoulders, the TE snaps his head and drives his outside arm across his body.
- Teach the TE that to do the "Lamborghini" means going full speed.

Lamborghini

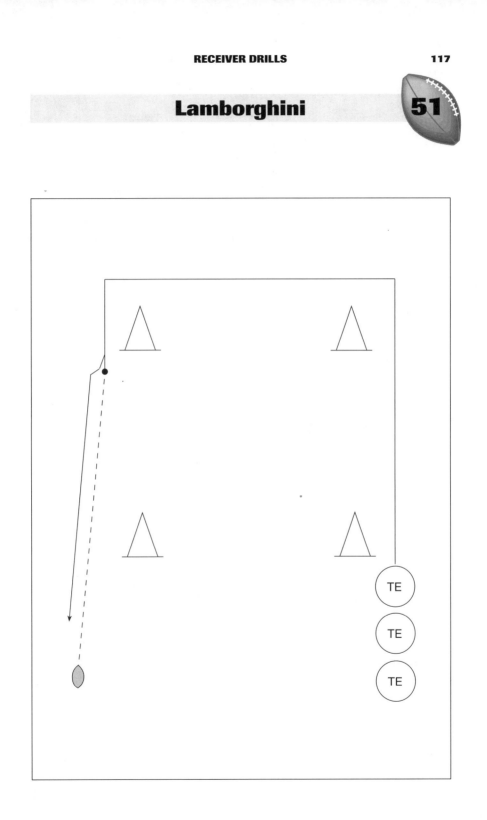

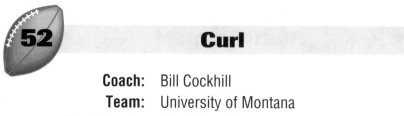

51

52   Curl

Coach: Bill Cockhill
Team: University of Montana
Head Coach: Mick Dennehy

Purpose: To teach receivers the need for consistency on pattern breaks.

Procedure:

1. One line of receivers align immediately inside cone #1.
2. Place cone #2 7 yards upfield as a landmark for the receiver.
3. Place cones #3 and #4 14 yards upfield.
4. On the snap, WR runs a curl-up route to and just before cone #2.
5. Next, the WR runs a stem to 14 yards and curls back between cones #3 and #4.
6. The QB drops back and throws the ball to the WR.

Key Points:

- Cones #1 and #2 control the starting and stopping points of a receiver.
- Cones #3 and #4 teach the receiver to create a good, consistent track back to the QB.
- The cones serve to set up good stem patterns such as curl, post, fade, or hitch-and-go.
- When ready, add a DB to push or align at the top end of the drill. Have the DB close and attempt to strip the ball.
- Teach the stopping techniques by having the WR come back to the ball on the break, lock the ball in (catch), tuck it away, and finish strong, five yards upfield.
- Run this drill at every practice to ensure consistency off the break.
- The coach may use different stems, but the breaks must be the same.

Curl

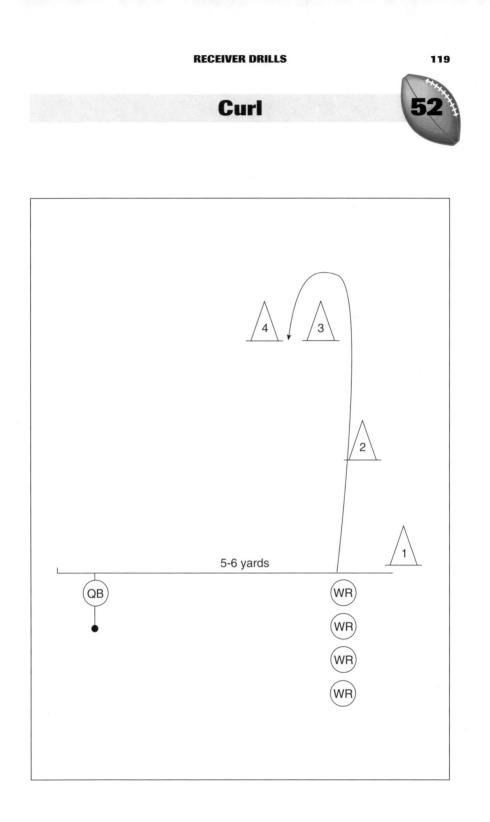

52

53   Fly-By

Coach: Kevin Faulkner
Team: University of New Mexico
Head Coach: Dennis Franchione

Purpose: To teach fundamentals of pass receiving.

Procedure:

1. Align two lines of receivers along the sideline area, 10 yards apart.
2. The coach (with four or five balls) stands near the middle of the two lines.
3. The line nearest the coach consists of defenders; the farther line consists of receivers. One defender aligns in a press technique in front of the first receiver.
4. On command, the receiver runs forward while a second defender runs by, flashing his hands in front of the receiver.
5. After flashing, the fly-by defender becomes the next press defender, and the current press defender goes to the end of the receiver line.
6. The coach throws the ball to the receiver, who catches the ball with his hands. The receiver returns the ball to the coach and goes to the end of the defender line.

Key Points:

- Proper warm up should precede this drill.
- The fly-by defender must not touch the ball while flashing his hands in front of the receiver.
- Monitor the intensity of the drill.
- Emphasize the receiver's concentration skills.
- Variation: The receiver runs an out or dig route, using the sideline.

Fly-By

53

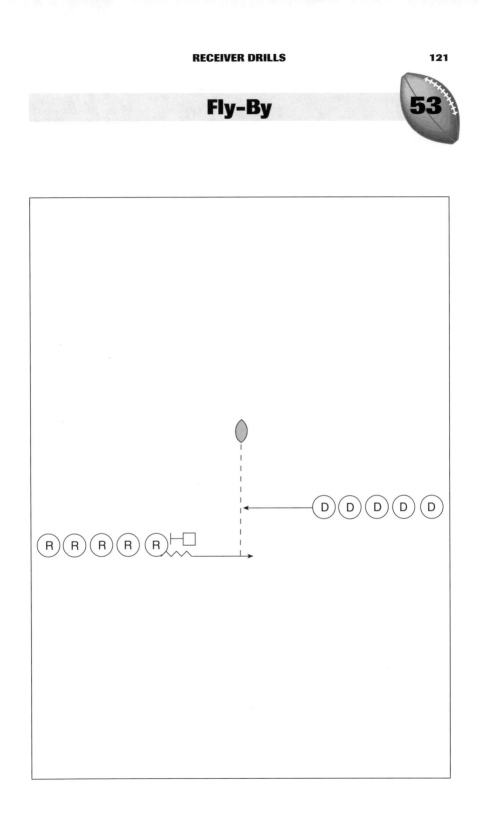

54   Pass Line

Coach: Martin Fine
Team: Indiana University
Head Coach: Cam Cameron

Purpose: To train receivers to attack the football and catch the ball with hands extended.

Procedure:

1. Starting 10 yards from the sideline, space three QBs (each with a ball) on a yard line, 10 yards apart across the field. Two other QBs (also with a football) are 20 yards downfield, facing them in a staggered position.
2. A line of receivers aligns at the sideline, 10 yards in front of the QBs.
3. On command, the first receiver turns around with hands extended and catches the ball thrown by the first QB.
4. The receiver then runs a straight line across the field, catching footballs on alternate sides from the QBs.
5. As the receiver catches the ball, he flips it back to the same QB who threw it to him.

Key Points:

- Station a coach at each sideline to ensure each receiver catches the ball with his hands extended.
- The QB must lead the receiver so he can run through the drill.
- The receiver must not fade away or use his body to catch the ball.
- Perform the drill from both sidelines.
- The only time the ball is secured by the receiver is on the far sideline.

Pass Line

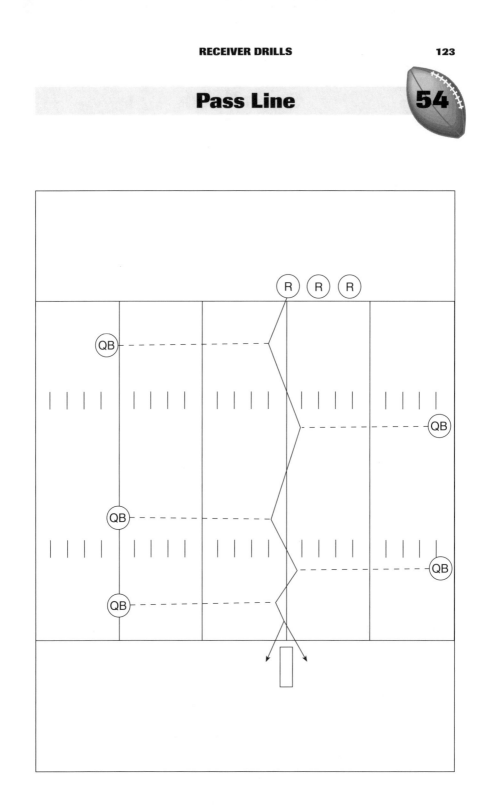

54

55   Great Catch

Coach: Mike Garrison
Team: University of Kansas
Head Coach: Terry Allen

Purpose: To improve WR foot technique on the sideline and end line.

Procedure:

1. Receivers align in a single file line facing the sideline.
2. The coach (with the ball) positions himself away from the WR so he can throw the ball to the first receiver in line.
3. On command, the WR runs toward the sideline to run the out, comeback, and corner route in that order.
4. The ball is thrown just out of bounds, short, low, or high, and the receiver catches with one hand on the sideline.
5. Repeat the throws. The receiver catches with two hands.
6. The coach moves behind the WR and throws ball over the WR's shoulder. The WR catches the ball with one or two hands.

Key Points:

- This drill is designed to work the top portion of the routes that ask receivers to make great catches wherever the ball is thrown.
- Stress proper footwork throughout the drill. Teach the WR how to use quick feet to ensure that one foot comes down inside the sideline without looking for the line.
- Encourage one-hand catches with control and look for perfection of the route at the finish.
- This drill takes only a small area, which cuts down on running and focuses more attention on catching and footwork.
- Variation: The WR executes a "dead leg" drag while catching the ball.

Great Catch

55

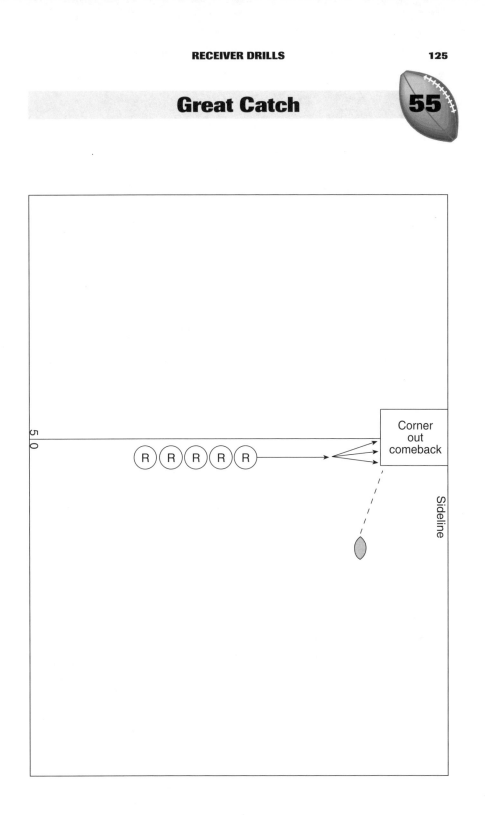

56 **Pass Gauntlet**

Coach: Greg Gatlin
Team: College of Siskiyous (California)
Head Coach: Greg Gatlin

Purpose: To teach receivers to catch the ball from different angles while on the move.

Procedure:
1. The teaching station extends from the goal line to the 40-yard line, and from the sideline to the near hashmark.
2. Two QBs (with two balls each) align near the sideline on the 20- and 40-yard lines, and two more QBs (also with two balls each) align facing them on hashmarks at the 10- and 30-yard lines.
3. One line of receivers aligns on the goal line, midway between the sideline and the hashmark.
4. The drill starts with the first receiver running forward, ready to catch a ball thrown by one of the four QBs. Receivers follow at 5-yard intervals to run the gauntlet.
5. After the catch, the receiver sprints past the 40-yard line, then circles back to the QB on the same side to return the football.

Key Points:
- At every 10-yard interval, the receiver turns his head quickly in the direction of that QB prepared to catch a pass. If the QB does not throw to him, he continues running to the next QB.
- Once the receiver has caught the ball, he tucks the ball away and sprints past the 40-yard line without looking at another QB.
- To avoid wasting time, the receiver returns the ball to the QB on the same side as the catch as quickly as possible, then gets back in line.
- Stress turning the head quickly and catching the ball with the hands.

Pass Gauntlet

56

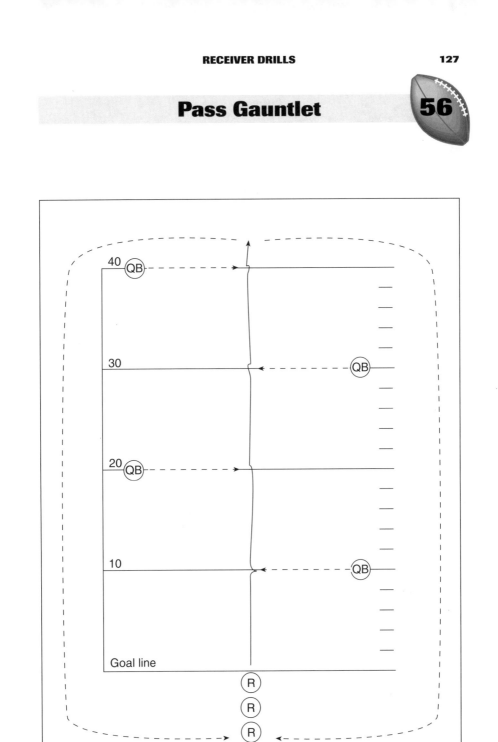

57

Vision

Coach: Dirk Koetter
Team: University of Oregon
Head Coach: Mike Bellotti

Purpose: To increase receiver concentration and demonstrate how much vision they really have to catch the ball with their eyes.

Procedure:

1. Each receiver places an eye patch or headband over one eye.
2. Give each receiver a designated route or have them work horizontally or vertically on a line.
3. The QB or coach (with ball) aligns 10 to 15 yards away from a line of receivers who are running horizontal lines.
4. On command, the receiver runs the line to catch a side bullet pass thrown by the QB.
5. The receiver catches the ball, secures it with proper leverage, then bursts upfield.
6. After the burst upfield, the receiver either returns to the end of the line or starts a new line on the opposite side.
7. Switch the eye patch to the other eye and repeat or take off eye patch and repeat.

Key Points:

- Catching the ball with one "big" eye forces the receiver to see the ball all the way into his hands and tuck.
- The QB (or coach) can throw the ball to certain spots to work on individual receivers' weak points (e.g., high balls).
- After removing the eye patch, emphasize how much more vision the receiver has and how vision and awareness can make him a better player.

Vision

- Variations:
  a. Add different types of catches.
  b. Vary which eye is covered.

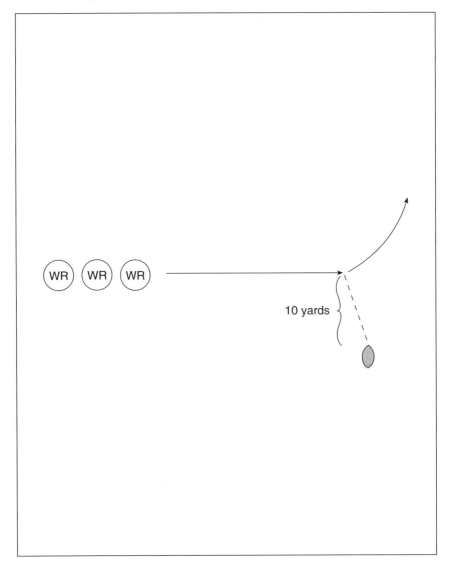

58   Fit-Ladder

Coach: Mike Mahoney
Team: St. Lawrence University
Head Coach: Dennis Riccio

Purpose: To establish proper stalk-blocking techniques for TEs and WRs in a ladder perimeter blocking scheme.

Procedure:

1. The TE and WR align two yards downfield in an offset position, away from the sideline.
2. Each receiver maintains outside leverage on a defender who is two yards away.
3. At the line of scrimmage, the QB pitches the ball to a RB, who attacks upfield, reading the block of the TE.
4. On the first whistle, the TE stalk-blocks his defender.
5. After clearing the TE's block, the RB continues up the ladder to the WR's block.
6. On the second whistle, the WR stalk-blocks his defender.

Key Points:

- Teach the technical breakdown of the stalk block prior to the drill.
- Each defender must attempt to contact the RB.
- While engaged in a stalk block technique, each player should be in a squat position with shoulders square, chin and shoulders back, and arms extended to the defender's sternum.
- The receiver maintains outside leverage by continuously shuffling his feet.
- Run the drill slowly or at full speed.

Fit-Ladder

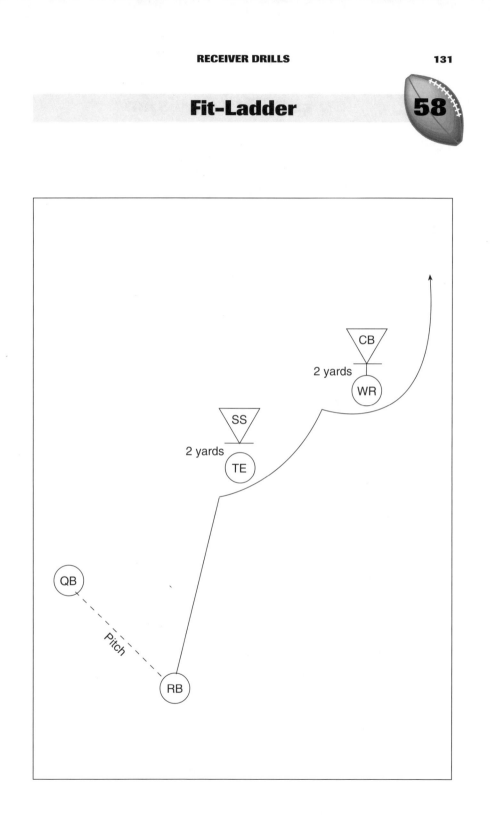

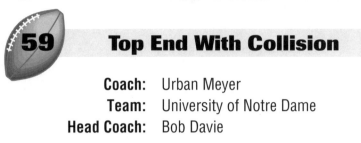

58

59   Top End With Collision

Coach: Urban Meyer
Team: University of Notre Dame
Head Coach: Bob Davie

Purpose: To teach receivers to concentrate, secure the ball, and get their pads down upon contact at the top end of their routes.

Procedure:

1. Place three cones downfield to mark the last eight yards of a curl route (see diagram).

2. Place two managers, each holding a blocking shield, at the end of the curl route.

3. To begin the drill, the receiver runs his route by going through the cones, working to plant and drive out of his cut.

4. Throw the ball as the receiver comes out of his break. As soon as he catches the ball, the managers swing their shields, attempting to dislodge the ball from the receiver.

5. After the collision, the receiver accelerates upfield.

Key Points:

- On the curl route, the receiver must lean and punch to the outside, then burst to the post. He then plants and drives back to the QB to catch the ball.

- This drill emphasizes ball security by having the receiver catch the ball in his hands, tuck it away immediately to avoid the assistants' shields, and burst upfield.

- Keeping the same managers creates a competitive drill and ensures that the bags are swung equally.

- Receivers should lower their pads on contact, which will help them break through tackles.

- Variations:

  a. Incorporate other routes.

  b. Change each day to a different route.

Top End With Collision

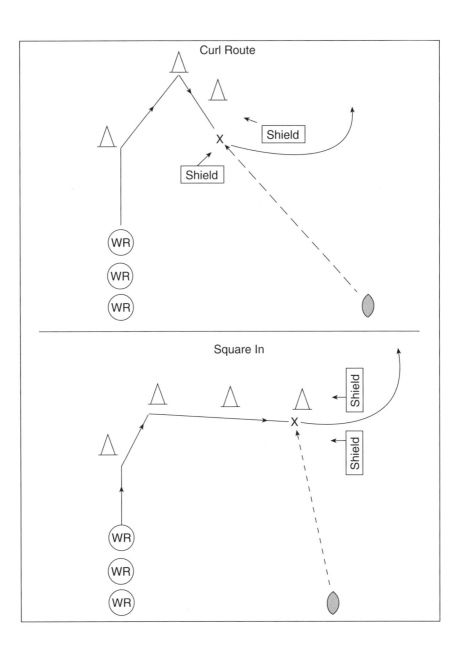

59

60   Distraction

Coach: Kirk Parrish
Team: Texas A&M
Head Coach: R.C. Slocum

Purpose: To teach receivers to catch the football while being distracted.

Procedure:

1. Divide the receivers into two lines, facing each other, 10 yards apart.
2. Designate one line as receivers and the other line as distracters.
3. The coach (with the ball) aligns in the middle of the two lines, 10 yards downfield.
4. To start the drill, one receiver and one distracter run toward each other. Throw the ball to the receiver over the head of the distracter as they pass each other.
5. The receiver must catch the ball with his hands.
6. After the catch, the receiver tucks the ball away securely, then runs to the end of the distracter line.
7. The distracter runs to the end of the receiver line.

Key Points:

- The distracter passes in front of the receiver with his hands up in the air.
- This drill is good for WRs, TEs, and RBs who need practice catching the ball in traffic.
- The receiver catches the ball as high as possible, using his fingertips.
- Stress that the receiver must focus on the football, not the distracter.

Distraction

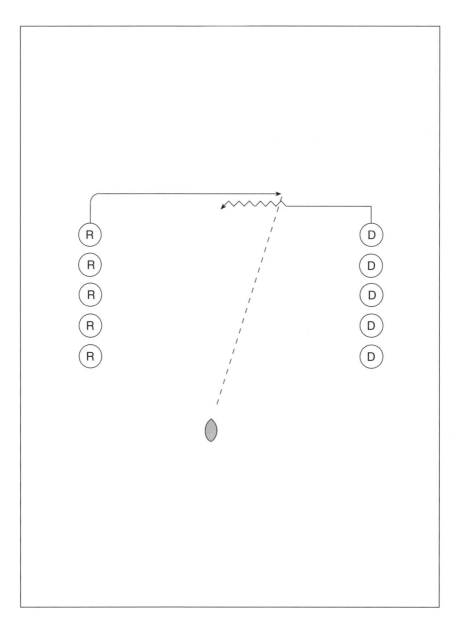

61   Towel

Coach: Don Patterson
College: University of Iowa
Head Coach: Hayden Fry

Purpose: To teach WRs proper stalk block techniques.

Procedure:

1. Pair up WRs with CBs. Set the CB across a line of scrimmage from the WR.
2. A coach with a towel aligns near the WR on the line of scrimmage.
3. Huddle with the WR and designate a running play and snap count. Both players assume proper stances and move on the snap count.
4. As the WR releases off the line of scrimmage, indicate the ball carrier's position by tossing a towel onto the field.
5. The CB takes the appropriate drop, then attacks the ball carrier (towel), while the WR uses stalk blocks to keep the CB from touching the towel.
6. The drill ends when the CB touches the towel or when the coach blows the whistle.

Key Points:

- The huddle call allows the WR to recognize proper block positioning for traps, dives, counters, draws, and other plays.
- WR must maintain a good base, slide into position, and focus on the defender's sternum while executing the stalk block.
- WR should not overextend, cross his feet, or look at the defender's head and shoulders while learning the technique.
- Stress that the WR take great pride in being able to tie up the defender until the whistle.

Towel

- Match up players by ability and rotate positions.
- Conduct the drill so the WR works both the left and right side.

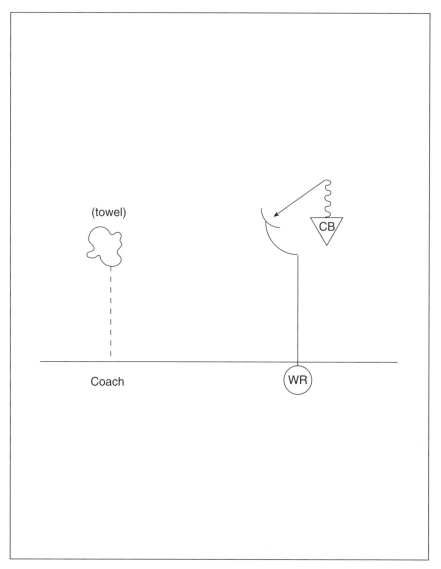

62   Cones—Burst

Coach: John Shannon
Team: Jackson State University
Head Coach: James Carson

Purpose: To improve the foot quickness and balance of receivers so, within a route, they can stop and come back to the QB.

Procedure:

1. The teaching station is a 10-yard square, with one cone in each corner and one cone in the middle of the square.

2. Place two square bags at a 45-degree angle at the far corners and another bag at one near corner to prevent the receiver from taking false steps.

3. One coach stands behind each far-corner bag, while an assistant (with the ball) is stationed at the front starting cone.

4. On command, the receiver sprints to each cone, stopping to redirect with only three steps.

5. When the receiver exits the last cone, the assistant throws the ball to him.

Key Points:

- When attacking the cones, the receiver must run full speed to simulate game-like conditions.

- To stop quickly and change direction, the receiver drops his center of gravity over his toes and executes the cut on the third step with his outside foot.

- The downfield coaches should correct the stop and come-back technique.

Cones—Burst

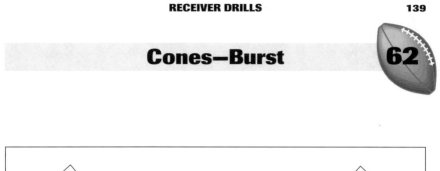

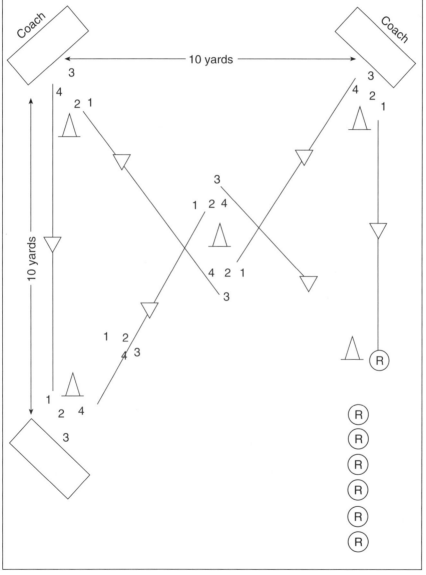

63   The Square

Coach: Pat Shurmur
Team: Michigan State University
Head Coach: Nick Saban

Purpose: To develop the TE's ability to break right and left while controlling his body position.

Procedure:

1. Place four cones at the corners of a square, 10 yards on a side.
2. TEs align in a single file behind one cone, with the first TE in a three-point stance.
3. Place a defender at the first, second, and third cones to harass the TE when he is running the square.
4. The coach (with ball) aligns on the line of scrimmage in the middle of the side.
5. The drill starts when the TE releases from the line of scrimmage, avoids the first defender, and sprints to the second cone.
6. As he approaches the second cone, the TE avoids another defender, then breaks around the cone.
7. While sprinting to the third cone, the TE avoids the third defender, then breaks around the cone.
8. At this last break, throw the ball to the TE, who makes the catch, tucks the ball away, and finishes by sprinting past the fourth cone.

Key Points:

- While sprinting, the TE must keep his weight down, arms pumping, and body under control.
- On the last break, the TE must pull his head and shoulders around sharply while extending his arms out to catch the ball away from his body.
- The TE must catch the ball with his hands or risk a defender plucking it away.

The Square

- Teach two break techniques:
  a. "Speed" breaks plant the off foot in the direction of the break.
  b. "Squared" breaks plant the off foot opposite the direction of the break.
- Practice both speed and squared breaks in each direction.

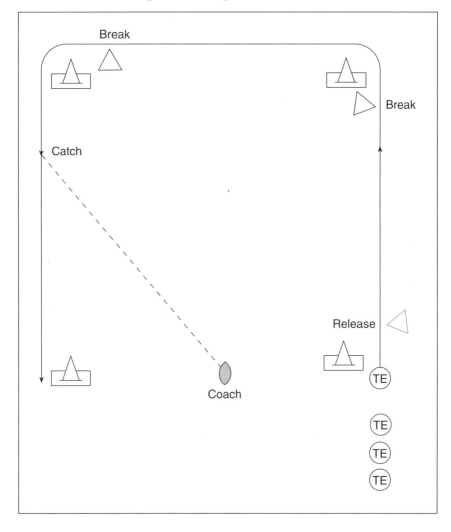

PART 5

Team Drills

Courtesy of University of Maryland

Position-specific drills are an important part of your players' development. Linemen need to work on run- and pass-blocking technique. Running backs must perfect their starts, agility, ball-carrying, blocking, and pass-receiving skills. Quarterbacks need to work on their footwork, fakes, drops, throwing mechanics, and decision making. Receivers concentrate on their pass routes, blocking, and pass-catching technique.

At some point, however, all this individual skill work performed in drills must be put into the team framework. An offensive squad is successful only if its players perform as an integrated unit.

Execution is the name of the game. And most coaches agree that repetition is the only way for a team to master the execution of plays. Imagine how many times the University of Southern California offense practiced the tailback pitch-sweep during the '70s. And wouldn't you like a dollar for every time Brigham Young University's offense has worked on its array of pass plays?

The offensive squad shouldn't limit team practices to only plays from its basic system. Its drills should also prepare it for specific game situations and opponent's strengths and tendencies as well as develop team-wide attributes that will enhance the unit's performance. In this section of the book, you're sure to find several drills that will improve both the physical and mental preparation of your offensive squad. Use them and see what a difference it makes on the scoreboard.

Team Drills

Drill	Coach	Team
64 Openers	Al Borges	UCLA
65 Perimeter Team	Dave Cutcliffe	Tennessee
66 Concentration	Gene Dahlquist	Texas
67 Halfline	Dan Dorazio	Boston University
68 Scramble	Doc Holliday	West Virginia
69 West Point	Herb Meyer	El Camino H.S. (CA)
70 Half Line	Bob Noblitt	U.S. Air Force Academy
71 Pass Pattern Polish Against Air	John Reaves	South Carolina
72 Chair	Rowland "Red" Smith	Jesuit H.S. (CA)
73 Team Takeoff	Morris Watts	Louisiana State
74 Buck Sweep	Walter Wells	Eastern Kentucky
75 Blitz Read and Pickup	Scott Westering	Pacific Lutheran University

64   Openers

Coach:	Al Borges
Team:	UCLA
Head Coach:	Bob Toledo

Purpose: To practice the opening 20 plays in the game plan.

Procedure:

1. The defensive scout team huddles at the line of scrimmage, breaks its huddle, and aligns in the defense called.
2. The starting offensive team huddles, and the QB receives the play from the sideline, makes the call, brings the team to the line, and executes the play.
3. Substitute players practice entering the game from the sideline.
4. To simulate game conditions, keep a 25-second clock.

Key Points:

- The signaler and play caller relay the play from the sideline to the QB on the field as under game conditions.
- According to the play called, substitutes enter and leave the field.
- Teach the QB to audible within the time limit.
- The 20 plays concern only first- and second-down calls.
- This drill should be part of every offensive game plan.

Openers

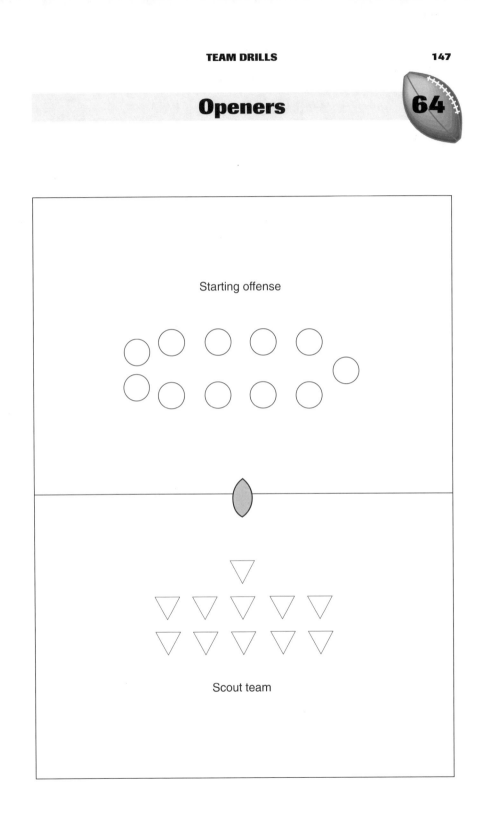

64

Starting offense

Scout team

65   Perimeter Team

Coach: Dave Cutcliffe
Team: University of Tennessee
Head Coach: Phil Fulmer

Purpose: To improve the execution of screens and special plays.

Procedure:
1. Set up a defensive scout team, using speedy players.
2. Two offensive teams huddle and alternate running plays from a script.
3. The running back, offensive line, and receiver coaches align on the defensive side to coach the scout team.
4. On the snap, the first offense executes the play. The defense reacts and returns quickly to defend the second offense, which runs the same play.

Key Points:
- If you have to increase the defensive line's unit speed, use smaller, quicker players.
- During the drill, have the defense work off a specific script (detailed action and reaction) to ensure that defenders run and react according to the call.
- The offense should run 14 plays in 10 minutes.
- Begin the drill early in practice when players are fresher.
- Insist the drill be executed under game-like conditions (with a clock).
- Since screens and special plays take a while to develop, all players must hustle.
- Keep in mind that a defender's reaction time to a given play is difficult to recreate.

Perimeter Team

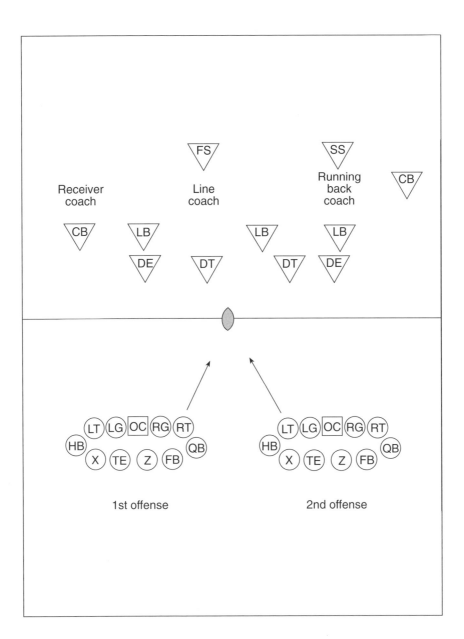

65

1st offense   2nd offense

Concentration

Coach: Gene Dahlquist
Team: University of Texas
Head Coach: John Mackovic

Purpose: To teach the offensive team to concentrate on good execution during pressure situations.

Procedure:

1. Three offensive units rotate executing plays from their five-yard line into the end zone.

2. One coach aligns on the goal line. He judges the success or failure of each play and spots the ball.

3. Three coaches align apart from each other in front of the offense to provide as much noise and distraction as possible.

4. To start the drill, unit #1 huddles, breaks to the line of scrimmage, and executes the called play. To be judged successful, all players must sprint through the end zone. Units #2 and #3 prepare to repeat the drill.

5. A successful play gives that offensive unit a one-yard gain on its next spot, but a failed play results in a one-yard loss on the next spot.

Key Points:

• The coaching checklist includes the following:

 a. Each unit breaks to the line of scrimmage from a disciplined huddle.

 b. Each unit uses changes in the snap count, setting up shifts and motion.

 c. Each unit properly uses audibles or "check with me " procedures.

• Linemen must pull and run as dictated by the play call, including screens and draws.

• Players not involved in the drill stand at the one-yard line and attempt to drown out the QB's cadence.

Concentration

66

- The drill lasts 5 to 10 minutes, which is enough time to establish team effort and execution in an intense pressure situation.

- Insist that each unit concentrate on moving together and running the play exactly as designed.

- For each successful play the teams may earn a rest break. For not executing a play correctly there could be some form of punishment.

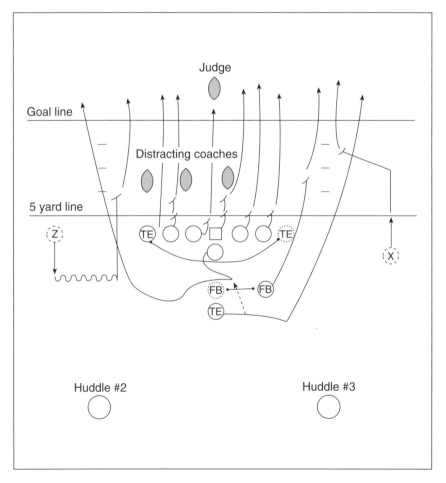

67   Halfline

Coach: Dan Dorazio
Team: Boston University
Head Coach: Tom Masella

Purpose: To drill the offense to perfect the outside running attack.

Procedure:

1. The offensive unit consists of OC, OG, OT, a perimeter blocker (TE, FL, or WR), and a complete backfield.
2. The defense has six defenders (DT, DE, two LBs, CB, and S) ready to stop the outside attack.
3. On the snap, run a scripted play to the right and the defense reacts.
4. At the same time, a companion drill involves the other side in some phase of the offense.
5. After 12 minutes, change so the other side of the line has its turn running outside plays.

Key Points:

- The drill is best run off scripted plays against a specific defensive set.
- Enhance the drill by having the defense work on their skills.
- Give special attention to correct footwork, backfield mesh points and routes, and proper targets in blocking techniques.
- To ensure maximum repetitions, run all plays against a single defensive look.
- Perform the drill either live or with each defender holding a bag.

Halfline

67

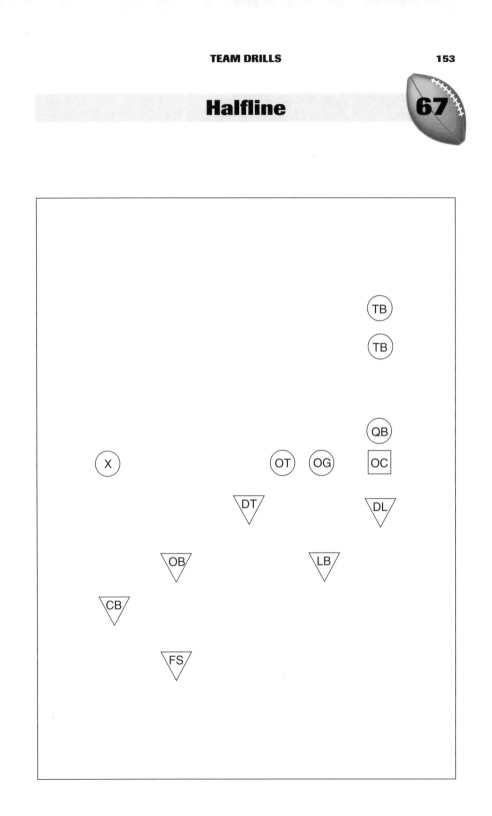

68   Scramble

Coach: Doc Holliday
Team: West Virginia
Head Coach: Don Nehlen

Purpose: To teach the QB and receivers how to execute a pass play while the QB scrambles.

Procedure:
1. The defensive scout team and offensive team come together for a skeleton passing drill.
2. Prior to practice, write up scripts of plays and coverages.
3. On the snap, the QB drops back to pass. Periodically, the offensive coach commands the QB to scramble.
4. When the QB hears the scramble command, he escapes by breaking out of the pocket to either his right or left.
5. When they see the QB scramble, all receivers apply their scramble rules.
6. While scrambling, the QB identifies and throws to an open receiver.

Key Points:
- The QB's scramble techniques and receivers' scramble rules are practiced prior to the drill.
- Prior to the drill, receivers practice individual techniques and learn their scramble rules.
- Receiver scramble rules are as follows:
  a. To the scramble side, receivers work outside with the QB movement, staying on their level (deep, short, or intermediate). A receiver who is pinned on the sideline turns downfield.
  b. Away from the scramble side, all receivers work toward the QB's movement and stay aware of receivers on the scramble side. They work different levels, and the deepest receiver stays deep while working across the field.
- All receivers work aggressively to get open, stay in the QB's vision, and spread the field without bunching up.

Scramble

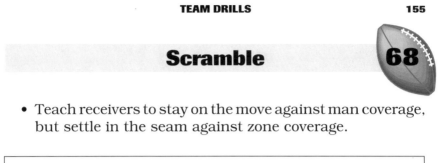

- Teach receivers to stay on the move against man coverage, but settle in the seam against zone coverage.

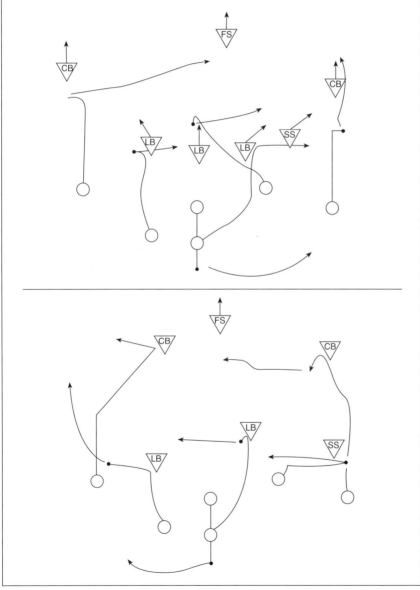

69   West Point

Coach: Herb Meyer
Team: El Camino High School (Califiornia)
Head Coach: Herb Meyer

Purpose: To teach linemen to fire out and drive-block and teach backs to block or read the linemen's blocks by running to daylight.

Procedure:

1. Create three chutes by placing four bags on the ground parallel to each other, two yards apart.
2. One offensive lineman and one defensive lineman or LB align on opposite ends of each chute.
3. Place a RB behind each blocker.
4. On the snap, the QB pivots and hands off the ball to one of the three RBs, who runs a dive play.
5. The RB who receives the handoff reads the block and runs to daylight. The other RBs join the lineman in their chutes to execute double-team blocks.

Key Points:

- Each offensive lineman attacks the defender and takes him using any run-blocking technique.
- QB signals the FB (middle chute) to run to either his right or left side.
- The QB chooses which back will be the ball carrier.
- Emphasize that a RB who is not the ball carrier must help the offensive lineman in his chute block the defender.
- Conduct this competitive drill at full speed.

West Point

69

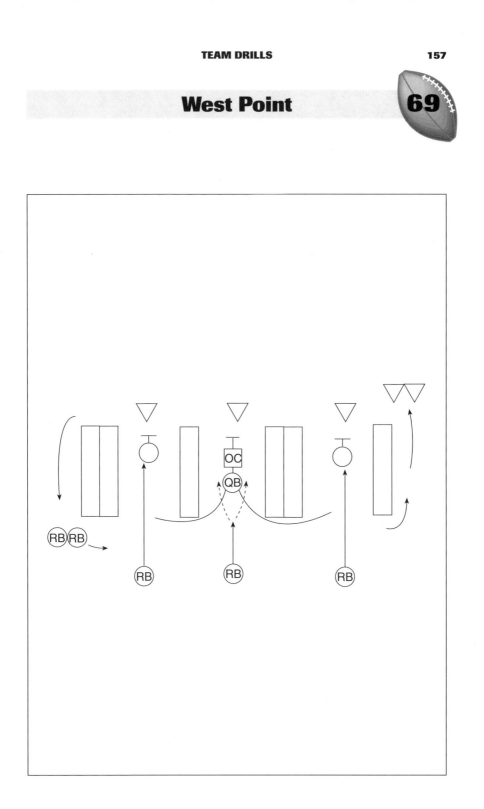

70   Half Line

Coach: Bob Noblitt
Team: U.S. Air Force Academy
Head Coach: Fisher DeBerry

Purpose: To increase the number of live playside repetitions for teaching the triple option and action passes.

Procedure:

1. An offensive team aligns on the hashmark, including two centers, two QBs, and two FBs.

2. The defensive team aligns opposite, including a second FS.

3. On the snap, the offense alternately attacks toward the wide and the narrow boundary sides of the field.

4. By alternating direction, the defense has time to realign.

5. Depending on the time available, call plays either in the huddle or at the line of scrimmage.

Key Points:

- By going full speed, the QB gets realistic reads, the offensive line practices correct blocking assignments, and receivers practice route timing.

- During motion (SB and WB) to playside, be sure to keep motion paths clear of other players who are setting up.

- Insist that all defenders align properly, based on the defensive call.

- The coach can script both the offensive plays and defenses to save practice time. Scripting also allows the coaches to be aware of what to expect.

- Conduct this competitive drill from either hashmark.

Half Line

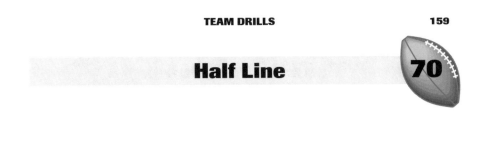

70

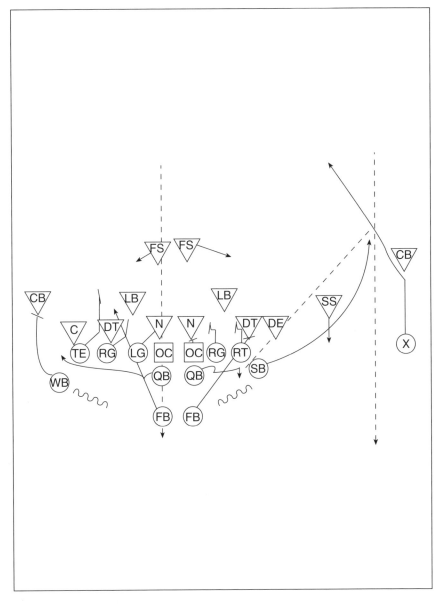

Pass Pattern Polish Against Air

Coach: John Reaves
Team: University of South Carolina
Head Coach: Brad Scott

Purpose: To teach WRs and backs to run correct patterns against various coverages.

Procedure:

1. The OC places the ball on the right hashmark, ready for play.

2. The SE (X) aligns in normal split on the boundary side; a flexed TE (Y) aligns 2 yards inside the left hashmark; and the flanker (Z) aligns off line of scrimmage, between left hashmark and field numbers.

3. The FB aligns 4.5 yards behind the RT, and the TB aligns 4.5 yards behind the LT.

4. On the snap, the QB executes a five-step drop.

5. The receivers run the following routes:

   a. X runs a 12-yard square out.

   b. Y runs a 12-yard post.

   c. Z runs a 12-yard square out.

   d. FB runs a 5-yard hook inside and 3 yards outside the RT.

   e. TB runs a 5-yard delay over the LT.

6. Rotate three units, each with a QB, three WRs, and two RBs. Each unit progresses as follows:

   a. First group up, QB throws to Z (square out).

   b. Second group up, QB throws to Y (post).

   c. Third group up, QB throws to X (square out).

   d. First group up, QB throws to TB (delay).

   e. Second group up, QB throws to FB (hook).

Pass Pattern Polish Against Air

71

Key Points:

- The groups line up behind each other and run patterns in rapid succession.
- Each position coach checks his players for proper depth, techniques, and mechanics in executing each pattern.
- Insist upon a 100 percent completion rate.
- Coaches tell receivers what coverage they can expect before the snap.

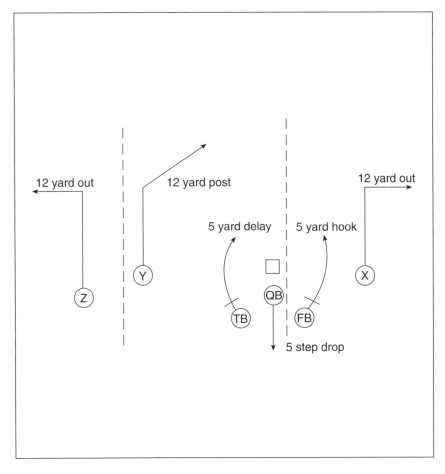

72   **Chair**

Coach: Rowland "Red" Smith
Team: Jesuit High School (California)
Head Coach: Dan Carmazzi

Purpose: To mentally test the offensive line on their blocking rules against a given opponent.

Procedure:

1. The offensive line sits side by side on turned-around folding chairs. Each player sits with his forearms on the chair back, his head down on his arms. Include the TE if necessary. The QB sits behind the offensive line.

2. Eight defensive players sit on folding chairs directly across from the offensive line, according to the opponent's anticipated defense.

3. The coach stands behind the offense, ready to call formation, play, and snap count.

4. On the snap, the offense bring their heads up quickly and point to the defender they are to block.

5. The coach continually makes defensive adjustments.

6. Repeat play calling until you meet the team goals.

Key Points:

• This drill requires the offensive line to concentrate and focus on their game assignments.

• This drill is especially effective after the pregame meal or in extremely rainy conditions.

• This drill can cover many parts of the offense, including opening script plays, red-zone offense, minus goal line plays, and special plays.

• To ensure accuracy, make corrections immediately.

• This is an excellent drill to enhance play recognition in a short period of time.

Chair

- Variations:
  a. Include RBs and WRs who must block.
  b. Include pass protection.

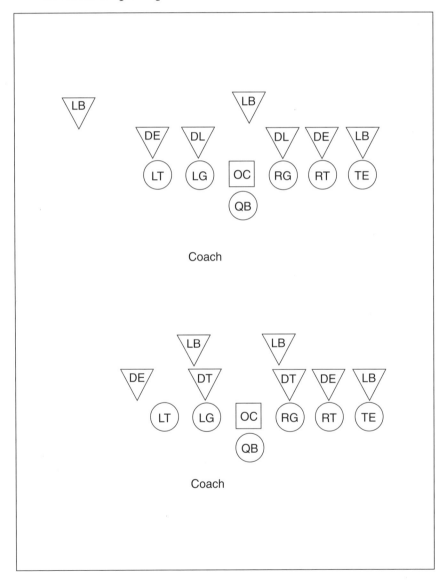

73   Team Takeoff

Coach:	Morris Watts
Team:	Louisiana State University
Head Coach:	Gerry DiNardo

Purpose: To start practice by emphasizing team execution in areas of need.

Procedure:

1. Run two offensive units against air, one on each hashmark.
2. One offensive unit breaks the huddle to align on the hashmark, ready to run a called play.
3. On the snap, the other unit calls its play, ready to alternate.
4. Coaches emphasize two areas of concern each day.

Key Points:

- Each practice, pick two concerns off this checklist:
  a. Huddle break
  b. Cadence and false cadence (work on snap count)
  c. Motions
  d. Shifts
  e. Run or pass checks (coaches call out the coverage or number in the box to the QB)
  f. Blitz checks (coaches call out the blitz look or defense)
  g. Two-minute drill (each unit takes four at a time)
- This is an excellent drill to start an offensive practice period.

Team Takeoff

73

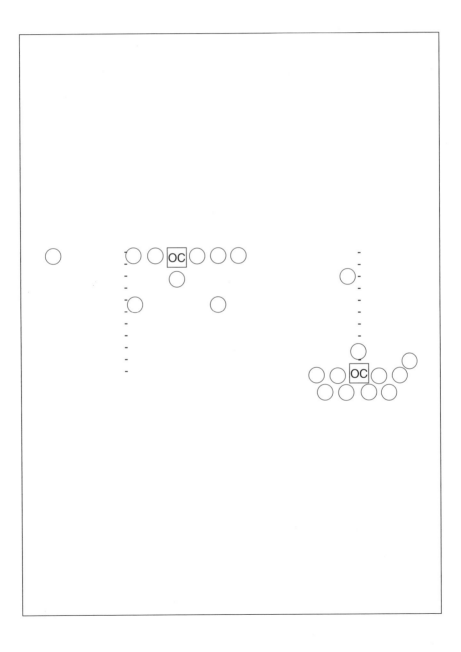

Buck Sweep

Coach: Walter Wells
Team: Eastern Kentucky University
Head Coach: Roy Kidd

Purpose: To teach guards the fundamentals of pulling coordinated with backfield action in running the buck sweep play.

Procedure:

1. Place two alignment hoses that have been marked with five offensive positions on the ground, side by side.

2. Place one cone 2.5 yards behind where the playside tackle would align, another cone behind where the WB would align in a wing-T formation.

3. Position five defenders (hand shields) in a defensive set.

4. Align an OC (with the ball) between and behind the hoses.

5. Align one OG on each side of the OC.

6. Position each RB to create a right or left wing-T formation.

7. On the coach's cadence and snap count, the players execute their blocking assignments.

Key Points:

- Correct every phase of the drill from alignment to stance.
- Insist that the guards do not tip off that they are going to pull.
- When pulling, emphasize that the guard must get his elbow around and gain depth quickly (around the cones).
- Coach the OC on proper technique for blocking the backside defensive lineman.
- Continue the drill until you are satisfied with the number of repetitions against each defensive set.
- This drill is run from both the right and left formations.

Buck Sweep

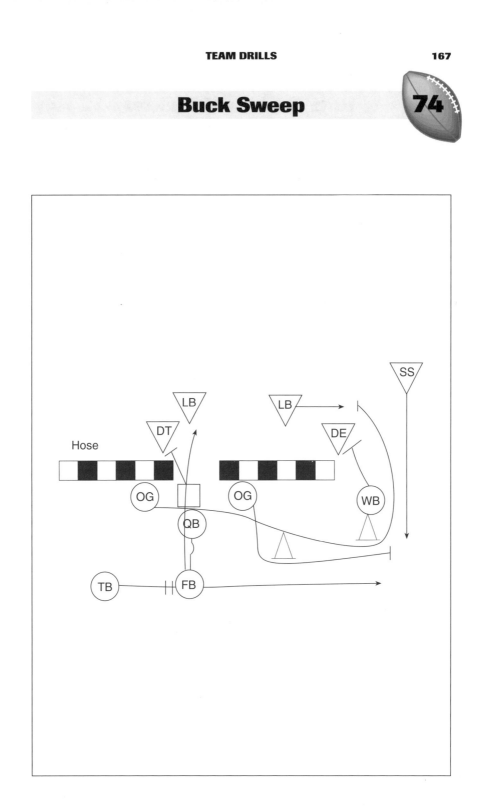

74

75   Blitz Read and Pickup

Coach: Scott Westering
Team: Pacific Lutheran University
Head Coach: Frosty Westering

Purpose: To teach all offensive players how to read basic blitzes.

Procedure:

1. The offensive unit aligns in for a called pass play while the defensive unit sets up on the ball.
2. The defensive unit prepares to stay basic or run a blitz package.
3. At the line of scrimmage, all offensive players identify and locate the alignment of the FS.
4. On the snap, the offense either runs the pass play with site adjustment or checks off to blitz routes.
5. On the snap, the defense stays basic or executes a blitz, and the offense reads and reacts.

Key Points:

- Offensive linemen must identify the field position of the FS.
- By identifying the FS's alignment, the team can be better prepared to block blitzes.
- To reinforce the read, the QB, backs, and receivers decide on their third step whether to react to a blitz.
- PSL (presnap look) is spoken in huddle to alert line of blitzes.

Blitz Read and Pickup

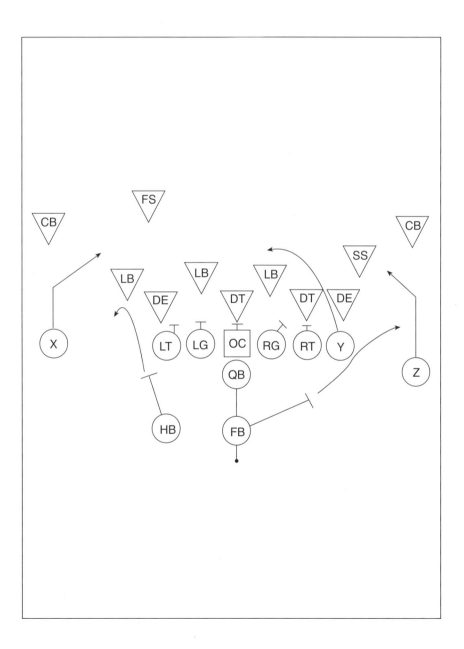

About the AFCA

Since its establishment in 1922, the American Football Coaches Association has striven to "provide a forum for the discussion and study of all matters pertaining to football and coaching" and to "maintain the highest possible standards in football and the coaching profession." These objectives, first declared by founders Alonzo Stagg, John Heisman, and others, have been instrumental in the AFCA's becoming the effective and highly respected organization it is today.

The AFCA now has more than 8,000 members, including coaches from Canada, Europe, Australia, Japan, and Russia. Through annual publications and several newsletters the Association keeps members informed of the most current rules changes and proposals, proper coaching methods, innovations in techniques, insights in coaching philosophy, and business conducted by the Board of Trustees and AFCA committees. A convention is held each January to give members a special opportunity to exchange ideas and recognize outstanding achievement.

The Association promotes safety in the sport and establishes strong ethical and moral codes that govern all aspects of football coaching. In addition, the AFCA is involved in numerous programs that ensure the integrity of the coaching profession and enhance the development of the game. It works closely with the National Collegiate Athletic Association, the National Association of Collegiate Directors of Athletics, the National Association of Interscholastic Athletics, the National Football League, the National Football Foundation and Hall of Fame, Pop Warner, and other organizations involved in the game of football. Indeed, one of the many goals of the Association is to build a strong coalition—TEAM AFCA—of football coaches who will speak out with a unified voice on issues that affect the sport and profession.

The AFCA is the team of the football coaching profession. All current and former football coaches or administrators involved with football are encouraged to join. To become a member of the American Football Coaches Association, please write or call

American Football Coaches Association
5900 Old McGregor Road
Waco, TX 76712
254-776-5900
http://www.afca.com/

More From the AFCA Series

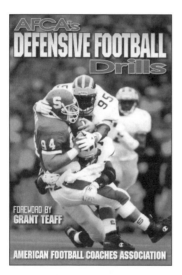

AFCA's Defensive Football Drills

American Football Coaches Association

Foreword by Grant Teaff

1996 • Paper • 168 pp
Item PAFC0476 • ISBN 0-88011-476-2
$15.95 ($23.95 Canadian)

Contains 70 innovative drills that develop
the fundamentals every defender needs
to compete in today's game. Features drills
and insights from many of football's fin-
est defensive coaches.

Football Coaching Strategies

American Football Coaches Association

Foreword by Grant Teaff

1995 • Paper • 216 pp
Item PAFC0869 • ISBN 0-87322-869-3
$18.95 ($28.95 Canadian)

All-time great coaches at all levels cover
every crucial aspect of the game including 28 articles on offense; 19 on defense;
7 on special teams; and 13 on philosophy,
motivation, and management.

Human Kinetics Books Cover the Gridiron

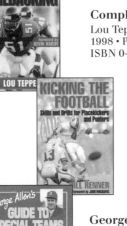

Complete Linebacking
Lou Tepper • Foreword by Kevin Hardy
1998 • Paper • 328 pp • Item PTEP0797
ISBN 0-88011-797-4 • $19.95 ($29.95 Canadian)

Kicking the Football
Bill Renner • Foreword by John Mackovic • 1997
Paper • 184 pp • Item PREN0685
ISBN 0-88011-685-4 • $16.95 ($24.95 Canadian)

George Allen's Guide to Special Teams
George H. Allen and Joseph G. Pacelli • Foreword by Dick
Vermeil • 1990 • Paper • 240 pp • Item PALL0370
ISBN 0-88011-370-7 • $19.95 ($27.95 Canadian)

Football's West Coast Offense
Frank Henderson and Mel Olson • Foreword by LaVell
Edwards • 1997 • Paper • 192 pp • Item PHEN0662
ISBN 0-88011-662-5 • $16.95 ($24.95 Canadian)

Football's Best Offensive Playbook
Dwight "Dee" Hawkes, Editor • Foreword by Dennis Erickson
1995 • Paper • 144 pp • Item PHAW0574 • ISBN 0-87322-574-0
$15.95 ($22.95 Canadian)

Coaching Football Successfully
Bob Reade • Foreword by Joe Paterno • 1994
Paper • 192 pp • Item PREA0518
ISBN 0-87322-518-X • $19.95 ($29.95 Canadian)